Sovereign

Duty

KrisAnne Hall, J.D.

Edited by Steve Andrews

ISBN-13:978-1499121148

DEDICATION

This book is dedicated to my friends and family. Without them I could not do any of this. To my son, without him, I'd lack proper motivation. To God, without Him, I can do nothing

CONTENTS

ACKNOWLEDGMENTS

Special Love and Thanks to Ignasio Aquavelva, EscapedNY, Annie the Anarchist, Jerry "the Director", Dan from Albuquerque, TR, Jack Rogers, Zak Carter, & last but not least, my fellow Anglo-History geek; Robin Keorner. You have all been there for me, when I needed you, above and beyond the call of duty. You are my Liberty First Generals.

FORWARD

"One morning after listening to your radio show I was praying for you, your family and this ministry; the Holy Spirit filled me with this image and sensation that illustrates what I see in your mission and how our Country is responding to it. I call it "Liberty's Whisper" because it is not meant for everyone to hear (at least not in the beginning) and also how rapidly a whisper can spread. But it also had an endearing purpose. In my family we often teased our vertically challenged members... saying they weren't much more than a whisper. As I've watched you grow in this ministry you've gone from a whisper to a rushing wind and the Liberty movement is growing stronger every day because of it. Thank you for all that you do!"

~ Judy Thacker

Liberty's Whisper

It started as a whisper, like a soft and subtle breeze,
    A rustling of some branches, the fluttering of leaves.
Many barely noticed, swiftly went on about their day;
    Tending to their business, hustling on their way.
And when the Remnant heard the distant words
    they felt the warm wind blow;
They paused and stopped and looked around,
    for far too few would know.
The message piercing and bittersweet,
    lingered heavy in the air.
But the Whisper only calls on those who really care to hear.
The whisper was a warning, pleading with all of man;
    Liberty is your gift from God and tyranny's at hand!
Then the whisper traveled like a rushing wind,
    growing stronger everyday
Until many had heard the whisper, and what it had to say.
It called on Man to take a stand, whatever be their fate.
    Thy Kingdom come, thy will be done, we will not live
    as slaves!
The subtle breeze, the warm wind blow, the rushing new
day wind
    It is a force that stays the course, if we but trust in
    HIM!
Liberty can't end here, it can't end now, though the final
hour is near.
    We have the chance the circumstance to make our
    voices clear.
We reject a Revolution, we don't want violent change.
We only want our Constitution, though we will not bow in
chains.

    ~ Judy Thacker

Introduction

The gift of Liberty was purchased for us with great sacrifice. The men and women at our founding understood that Liberty is a gift from God and that all God's gifts are worth our every effort. John Adams, in a letter to his wife Abigail in 1777, reminds us of the charge we have to ensure that the gift of Liberty is not squandered.

"Posterity! you will never know how much it cost the present generation to preserve your freedom! I hope you will make a good use of it. If you do not, I shall repent in Heaven that I ever took half the pains to preserve it."[1]

We must heed the warnings of history and make every effort to pass on the gift of Liberty to future generations. We cannot do that if we *lose* our history. Too often history is revised in ways that demean America's founders and undermine America's foundation. By allowing lies to be taught to our sons and daughters, we dishonor those who gave so much, and Liberty is put in peril.

I am not trying to give the founders some divine status or even attribute to them a level of perfection that they did not have. John Adams himself had some serious lapses in judgment when it came to honoring his oath. We must understand that our nation was not founded upon people, but upon *principles*. The people that gave us our exceptional American principles were flawed vessels just like you and me. However, the amazing part of this history is that those flawed men understood that the foundation of an enduring nation must be Liberty and that Liberty is only maintained by a society grounded in a shared morality. Consider these words by Alexander Hamilton:

"Equal pains have been taken to deprave the morals as to extinguish the religion of the country [France], if indeed morality in a community can be separated from religion…The pious and moral weep over these scenes as a sepulcher destined to entomb all they revere and esteem.

The politician who loves liberty sees them with regret as a gulf that may swallow up the liberty to which he is devoted. He knows that morality overthrown (and morality must fall with religion), the terrors of despotism can alone curb the impetuous passions of man, and confine him within the bounds of social duty."[2]

Our founders knew that Liberty is a combination of two equally important parts – it is FREEDOM under the constraints of a SHARED MORALITY. Liberty cannot survive where there is pure freedom. Pure freedom is man doing whatever is right in his own mind regardless of what it does to others: cheat, lie, steal, murder. Pure freedom is chaos. At the same time, Liberty cannot survive with moral law alone. Moral law not mingled with freedom is theocracy. Theocracy in the hands of men is tyranny in the name of religion. Our founders attempted to give us this balance and secure the blessings of Liberty for us in our founding documents. When we abandon our founding documents and disregard our moral foundations as we are doing today, Liberty is put in peril.

Thomas Jefferson warned, *"Can the liberties of a nation be thought secure when we have removed their only firm basis, a conviction in the minds of the people that these liberties are a gift from God?"*[3]

Benjamin Franklin cautioned America's founders during the Constitutional Convention:

"In the beginning of the Contest with Great Britain, when we were sensible of danger, we had daily prayer in this room for Divine protection.... All of us who were engaged in the struggle must have observed frequent instances of Superintending Providence in our favor...have we now forgotten that powerful Friend? or do we imagine we no longer need His assistance?.... God Governs in the affairs of men. And if a sparrow cannot fall to the ground without His notice, is it probable that an empire can rise without His aid?"[4]

Patrick Henry said *"Three millions of people, armed in the holy cause of liberty, and in such a country as that which we possess, are invincible by any force which our enemy can send against us. Besides, sir, we shall not fight our battles alone. There is a just God who presides over the destinies of nations, and who will raise up friends to fight our battles for us."*[5]

Our founders had a strong sense of something greater than themselves. Thomas Jefferson reminds us that, *"We are not in a world ungoverned by the laws and the power of a Superior Agent. Our efforts are in His hand, and directed by it; and He will give them their effect in His own time."*[6]

Yet when man begins to amass almost god-like, unchecked power all sense of moral restraint is tossed aside. When such men have control over the mechanisms that shape society, namely government and its institutions, tyranny is the natural result. Our nation has been in a constant struggle to evermore expand the boundaries of Liberty while pushing back the tyranny of the power-hungry and the amoral. The battle rages still. Today the rising tides of apathy, corruption, greed, deceit and gross immorality threaten to overwhelm the bulwarks erected by our founders. It will take courageous and tireless efforts to return this nation to balance.

It has been because of the principles of freedom and morality that America with all of its imperfections has been the haven of rest when tyrants oppress their own. She has been the vineyard of innovation and opportunity. This is the nation that opens its arms to the tired, to the poor, to the oppressed, to the huddled masses yearning to breathe free. No other nation can claim this legacy, no other people have this birthright. This is the shining city upon a hill, and if we let the light go out there will be darkness for generations around the world. We must revive the knowledge of our nation's history and of its foundations. We need a revolution of the mind.

We need to learn anew that we have an exceptional nation where *"all men are created equal and endowed by their Creator with certain inalienable rights;"* a nation birthed by the principle that the power of the government is to be held BY the people and not where the government holds power OVER the people; a nation that believes the principle that says all are free to worship according to the dictates of their conscience, and all are equally free, *"Jews, Turks, pagans, AND Christians;"* a nation that has prospered based on the principle that ideas and hard work open the door to prosperity regardless of bloodline, skin color or social status; a nation that has remained free because the citizens maintain the right to defend self, property, and Liberty. This is the nation we are fighting for, an exceptional nation founded on exceptional principles. Those principles have been enshrined in our founding documents. If those documents are destroyed, the foundation is lost. If the foundation is lost, the whole structure crumbles under the weight of unbridled tyranny.

In the words of Daniel Webster, *"Is our Constitution worth preserving? Guard it as you would guard the seat of your life, guard it not only against the open blows of violence, but also against that spirit of change…Miracles do not cluster. That which has happened but once in six thousand years, cannot be expected to happen often. Such a government, once destroyed, would have a void to be filled, perhaps for centuries, with evolution and tumult, riot and despotism."[7]*

So in these difficult times, let us keep a "laser focus" on what is important. In this day it is so popular to denigrate America for every little flaw. Why not take back a bit of American Exceptionalism? Why not embrace what makes us different from every other nation on the globe? America is an exceptional nation because we are built on exceptional principles that were enshrined in our founding documents - principles of Liberty, freedom, morality, and equality as derived from our Creator. And these principles are STILL WORTH FIGHTING FOR!

PART I

More Lenient Measures

1. Over The Cliff

A man and his wife are touring the beautiful mountains of some exotic location. The man sits behind the wheel of his sturdy Recreational Vehicle, his wife busily snapping pictures in the passenger seat. Inexplicably, in spite of the numerous signs declaring ROAD CLOSED - DO NOT ENTER, the man veers onto a bumpy overgrown road and floors it!

The woman yells, "What are you doing? You just busted through that barricade!"

The man just smiles and says, "You can trust me."

As they climb the hill at breakneck speed, a sign zips past saying **Danger: 1,000 ft. Drop Ahead**.

The woman screams as she helplessly clutches the seatbelt. "Stop! We are going to die." She thinks she sees a bit of insanity flash across her husband's face.

Just before the RV launches over the edge the man just smiles and says, "I think we're fine, we just need more gas."

Does it feel sometimes like you're the screaming passenger and the folks behind the wheel of America seem to have gone stark raving mad? The road is out. The signs are ignored.

And their solutions? "We just need more revenue, we just need to be re-elected, we just need more power, we just need more time…" We just need more gas!

We are broke and the federal system is broken at every level. It's time somebody grabbed the wheel and hit the brakes.

Every single branch, regardless of the party in control, has failed us and has failed in its duty to uphold the Constitution.

First consider the failures of Congress:

With the self-restraint of the town drunk on a 3-day binge, Congress spends and spends, borrows and spends some more and ignores the restraints the framers enshrined in our founding documents.

Consider James Madison's characterization of one of the fundamental powers of the House of Representatives:

"The House of Representatives cannot only refuse, but they alone can propose, the supplies requisite for the support of the government…This power of the purse may, in fact, be regarded as the most complete and effectual weapon with which any constitution can arm the immediate Representatives of the people, for obtaining a redress of every grievance, and for carrying into effect every just and salutatory measure."[8]

Would the founders even recognize this Congress? Madison was referring to Article 1 section 7 of the Constitution as a means of keeping an out-of-control government from going over the cliff:

"All Bills for raising Revenue Shall originate in the House of Representatives; but the Senate may propose or concur with amendments as on other Bills."[9]

The House has the sole authority to fund or defund every federal program. The defunding of unconstitutional federal programs, as Madison stated, is a vital part of governmental checks and balances. If there had been an RV in Madison's day, he would have understood that it would be much harder to drive that beast over a cliff if it had no gas in the tank. There are serious consequences if we refuse these checks and allow unconstitutional federal programs to continue. What does Congress do instead? At best nothing. At worst pile on more tyrannical spending and expand unconstitutional federal power. The Affordable Care Act (ACA) is just as an example, asserts power never delegated and attacks Religious Liberty. It wreaks havoc on an already wrecked economy.

As a result of unchecked power, we are hovering on the brink of insolvency, and government dependency is at an all-time high. Unemployment and lack of productivity is now an accepted way of life, and the loss of individual Liberty is considered a cost of doing business. Welcome to the new America where Congress has failed to protect the purse!

Understand however, that we are dealing with UNNECESSARY FAILURE. We were warned of these very things: **1,000 ft. Drop Ahead!** Let Alexander Hamilton read his road sign from the grave:

"No legislative act, therefore, contrary to the Constitution, can be valid. To deny this, would be to affirm, that the deputy is greater than his principal; that the servant is above his master; that the representatives of the people are superior to the people themselves; that men acting by virtue of powers, may do not only what their powers do not authorize, but what they have forbid."[10]

Unfortunately that is exactly what we have today as Congress continually authorizes powers not permitted under the Constitution. We get a sweet smile and a "trust me" from the lunatics behind the wheel and we act like it's just a smooth drive in the countryside.

Meanwhile, we keep barreling headlong toward that cliff. And not just a fiscal cliff but a freedom cliff! Congress has failed not only in the arena of finances, but it has failed miserably in accountability and oversight. The bottom line is, when you have a Congress who sees ITSELF as superior to the Supreme Law of the Land, it is certainly not going to hold rogue executives accountable.

Case in point, on June 28, 2012, the House of Representatives found Attorney General Eric Holder guilty of criminal contempt by a vote of 255-67, for refusing to turn over documents tied to the Fast and Furious gun-running murders. The next action that is required of the

House by the Constitution is very clear and is contained in Article 2 section 4. This section is a directive upon Congress.

*"The President, Vice President, and all civil officers of the United States **SHALL BE** removed from office on impeachment for and conviction of, treason, bribery, or other high crimes and misdemeanors."*[1] *(emphasis mine)*

The requirements for Congress to file and complete articles of impeachment against AG Eric Holder are clear.

1. Eric Holder is a civil officer;

2. Criminal contempt, in the very least is a misdemeanor.

Upon these conditions being met, the Constitution States Eric Holder **SHALL BE** removed from office. That leaves no room for discussion; it must be done. But Congress has failed to remove Eric Holder and has, through this inaction, declared that

1. Congress need not comply with the demands of the Constitution, and

2. Civil officers need not comply with the law.

But in today's Congress, constitutional considerations are overridden by political considerations (a form of lawlessness), "trust us, we just need more gas."

Congress has failed to represent the people, failed to protect the purse, failed to follow the Constitution and failed to hold others constitutionally accountable. It is no wonder that such a corrupt and clueless Congress is so disliked (to say the least). The people's representatives act as if they are above the law and ignore the warnings of our framers. Congress has failed. **1,000 ft. Drop Ahead!**

Next, consider the failures of the judiciary.

The Judicial system doesn't follow the Constitution any better than the rest of the federal government. The very foundation of the problem is the fact that our legal education system is no better than our government K-12 system. Law schools no longer teach the Constitution. They teach Constitutional Law. If you are "fortunate" enough to attend Harvard Law any time after Supreme Court Justice Elena Kegan served as Dean, you won't even have to learn Constitutional Law. Ms. Kegan, who went from law clerk to political advisor to Law professor to Supreme Court Justice, felt it important to REMOVE Constitutional Law from Harvard's list of graduation requirements and replace it with International and Comparative Law classes. Is this the action of someone who values America's founding documents?

But even if you do take Constitutional Law in law school, this doesn't mean you'll actually *learn* the Constitution. Instead you'll learn precedent. Precedent essentially means that men and women in black robes know more about the Constitution than the men who wrote it. Our law students, who will become our lawyers, our judges, and our Supreme Court Justices, as a result learn that precedent is superior to the Supreme Law. We have fallen prey to a gradual and very destructive creep from the foundational principles that make America great.

Jefferson had this to say on the matter in a letter to C. Hammond, August 18, 1821:

"It has long however been my opinion, and I have never shrunk from its expression, (altho' I do not chuse to put it into a newspaper, nor, like a Priam in armour, offer myself it's champion) that the germ of dissolution of our federal government is in the constitution of the federal judiciary; an irresponsible body, (for impeachment is scarcely a scare-crow) working like gravity by night and by day, gaining a little to-day & a little tomorrow, and advancing it's noiseless step like a thief, over the field of jurisdiction, until all shall be usurped from the states, & the government of all be consolidated into one."[12]

Just as Jefferson feared, Supreme Courts have authorized the power of lawmaking through the sanction of federal regulations. They have upheld the authority of unconstitutional regulatory agencies who in turn usurp the power of the States. The courts themselves usurp the power of the States by sanctioning the federal government's control over powers reserved to the States.

A great example of this is individual voting requirements, a power reserved to the States through Article 1, Section 2, Clause 1 of the Constitution. Because of the gradual takeover of this arena by the federal government we are now at a place where our voting system is as corrupted and insecure as ever, and voter fraud is the order of the day. What apparently began as a move to combat injustice has become a tool to undermine the entire electoral system.

In another egregious example, the statists seized on what many saw as legitimate shortcomings in the healthcare arena and used it as an excuse to claim more unauthorized power in the federal system. The Supreme Court then upheld the Federal Healthcare mandates as a proper use of federal power. The Supreme Court has condoned this usurpation in spite of the absence of any enumerated power in the Constitution regarding healthcare or insurance. They have also ignored the clear warning of the writers of the Constitution.

Listen to what James Madison has to say about this court-sanctioned expansion of federal authority:

*"The powers delegated by the proposed Constitution to the federal government are **few and defined**. Those which remain in the State governments are numerous and indefinite…(federal powers) will be exercised principally on **external objects**, as war, peace, negotiation, and foreign commerce; with which the last the power of taxation will, for the most part, be connected… The powers reserved to the Several States will extend to all the objects which, in the ordinary course of affairs, concern the lives, liberties, and properties of the people, and the internal order, improvement and prosperity of the State."[13] (emphasis mine)*

Madison makes it very clear that "external," meaning primarily foreign duties, are the powers delegated to the federal government and everything else not expressly delegated – including healthcare – remains in the hands of the people through their States.

Unless someone grabs the wheel, law schools will continue to avoid teaching the purpose and meaning of the Articles of the Constitution, and instead will follow judges blindly over the cliff and teach the law school lemmings to do the same. Consequently, we will continue to abandon the limited and defined government our founders envisioned through the misguided "off-roading" of ignorant judges.

What may be shocking to us today is that many of our founders felt that the federal courts were a bastion of defense against federal overreach. They believed that the courts would preserve the principles embodied in the Supreme Law of the Land. In truth the courts have become just the opposite. They are some of the most egregious assailants against the people's Liberty. Perhaps the founders underestimated the magnitude of today's ignorance, greed and immorality. Nevertheless, just like the Congress, the federal courts have failed.

Finally, it will not be hard to convince anyone that the Executive Branch has no better record. As years have progressed, our executive branch has grown to look more and more like the executives of old who ruled in limited monarchies.

Executive agencies create law but call them regulations in an attempt to avoid a charge of violating separation of powers. They tax the people but call them "fines," resulting in a modern day manifestation of the grievance of "taxation without representation." Executive Orders are not used as they were intended; a rule making power for the executive branch **to govern its own departments**. Instead, President after President has used the power of Executive Order as a monarchial tool of decree. These orders write laws when Congress refuses, thus allowing the Executive Branch to follow its every whim and fancy without the consent of the governed.

Writing law, overturning law, and setting aside law without the consent of the Legislative Branch is an old tool used by tyrannical kings to destroy the liberties of the people. Take for example the list of grievances against King James II, written in the English Bill of Rights created in 1689. In one instance they accuse James of extirpating (completely destroying) Liberty.

"Whereas the late King James the Second, by the assistance of divers evil counsellors, judges and ministers employed by him, did endeavour to subvert and extirpate the Protestant religion and the laws and liberties of this kingdom; By assuming and exercising a power of dispensing with and suspending of laws and the execution of laws without consent of Parliament;"[14]

Even the people and their representatives of 1689 recognized such use of Executive Orders is the complete destruction of Liberty. Today's executive says, "trust me, I have a pen and a phone," and the legislature simply looks annoyed (or at least Daryl Issa does) and then just hangs on for the ride. 1,000 ft. Drop Ahead! Somebody better grab the wheel! In fact, we the people have a **responsibility** to grab the wheel!

Remember, Executive Orders were not intended to be constitutionally enforceable on the people but simply rule making procedures for the executive branch to manage its own internal operations. The problem is that Congress has given the executive branch the power to make law by setting up REGULATORY AGENCIES. Regulatory Agencies are executive branch agencies, established by the legislative branch, to be controlled by the executive branch. Through these executive agencies, Executive Orders are enforced upon us through regulatory "laws."

Executive orders are an unconstitutional use of legislative power either by the theft of power or by consent of Congress. It really doesn't matter how; the result is still the same. Because of separation of powers the president is not authorized constitutionally to write, set aside, or overturn LAW. That is a power delegated to the legislature. These regulatory agencies are unconstitutional entities. The federal government was never delegated the power to regulate INTERNAL affairs of the States in such a manner.

(See Fed. 45 and James Madison's explanation of limited federal power)

Just like in 1689, the Executive Branch's long-standing disregard for its own constitutional limitations is leading to the "extirpation" of today's Liberty. We have tolerated a long line of lunatics and madmen sitting behind the wheel in the Oval Office, just as we have in the Congress and in the courts. Government has expanded under EVERY SINGLE PRESIDENT in recent history. The Executive has disregarded the road signs of the founders and continued to careen toward the precipice. Our framers cast off a king for a President in order to avoid an imperial monarchy, but look where we're headed. Let's face it, the Executive Branch has failed.

So what are we to do? Dale Carnegie said, *"Any fool can criticize, condemn and complain – and most fools do."*[15] We recognize that all three branches of government have failed to maintain themselves within their limited capacity, so what is our solution to this problem? Are we but fools to complain and do nothing?

The solution is the same as it has always been. Government was never expected to maintain itself. Keeping the government in its limited capacity has always been the duty of the people.

"We hold these truths to be self-evident, that all men are created equal, that they are endowed by their Creator with certain unalienable Rights, that among these are Life, Liberty and the pursuit of

Happiness.--That to secure these rights, Governments are instituted among Men, deriving their just power from the consent of the governed, --That **whenever any Form of Government becomes destructive of these ends, it is the Right of the People to alter or to abolish it,** *and to institute new Government, laying its foundation on such principles and organizing its powers in such form, as to them shall seem most likely to effect their Safety and Happiness.*"[16] *(emphasis mine)*

When the government escapes its limits or when people walk in ignorance or apathy and let government off of its constitutional leash, it is "the right of the people to alter or abolish that form of government." The good news is that we are not a Kingdom. We are a Constitutional Republic. We have simply forgotten this fact. It has never changed, but those who would rule us prefer that we forget. Our only solution is NOT revolution and chopping off Kings' heads. We have Constitutional remedies to solve these problems peaceably. This may be the true genius of our founders; real working solutions to an out of control government problem. The key to those solutions lies in our Sovereign Duty!

2. State Sovereignty

One of the greatest attacks on our Republic has been the distortion of the very nature and framework of our governmental structure. Namely, the incorrect notion that the federal government is the supreme boss over the States. In truth it was not the central government, but the States who were intended to retain the most power in our Republic. The States reclaiming their power and putting the federal government back in its limited and defined box will be essential to restoring the proper balance of government.

The largest impediment to this key check on federal power is the level of ignorance and miseducation among the citizenry. Several fundamental truths are grossly distorted in the minds of modern Americans. First citizens do not understand the nature of the **States** and their relationship to the federal government. Secondly, we do not understand the nature of our **Constitution** and its relationship to the federal government...

In order to get a good grasp on these issues, we must get back to some basics.

In The Beginning

Approximately one month prior to the Declaration of Independence, on June 7, 1776 Richard Henry Lee proposed the Lee Resolution; a three step process for the

States to declare independence from Great Britain and become sovereign States. The declaration was very simple:

1. "That these united Colonies are and of Right ought to be free and independent States.

2. That they are absolved from all allegiance to the British Crown and that all political connection between them and the State of Great Britain is and ought to be, totally dissolved.

3. That measures should be immediately taken for procuring the assistance of foreign powers, and a confederation be formed to bond the colonies more closely together.[17]"

On July 2, 1776, twelve colonial delegations voted in favor of the Lee Resolution, with New York abstaining. John Adams wrote to Abigail Adams on July 3, 1776 and proclaimed,

"The Second Day of July 1776, will be the most memorable Epocha in the History of America."[18]

This history is important though it is rarely taught. On July 2, 1776, (not July 4, 1776) the colonies became "independent and free States."

It is relevant to recognize there is no mention of a central government in the Lee Resolution or in the Declaration of Independence which would follow. It is a matter of historical fact that the States existed **prior** to the federal government. Although this may seem logical, the fact that it is not actively taught allows many misapplications of the Constitution and many misunderstandings about the narrow scope of federal power in our governmental hierarchy. The States from the outset were independent, sovereign entities which would go on to be the CREATORS of the federal government. But, I am getting ahead of myself. Let's consider the very nature of the States. What exactly does it mean to be "a State"? Or more importantly what was it intended to mean in our Constitutional system?

Sovereign Independent States

In modern thought, when we hear the word "State", we naturally think Florida, Georgia, Texas, New York, etc. To Americans today, those names signify subdivisions of our nation, lesser political entities which are placed on a wrung below the federal government in our governmental hierarchy. In other words, the federal government is the boss who issues the orders that the States follow. But that is not how our framers thought of States. A review of the last paragraph of the Declaration of Independence gives us all the information we need to properly understand the difference between the modern misconception and the framer's intent.

"We, therefore, the Representatives of the united States of America, in General Congress, Assembled, appealing to the Supreme Judge of the world for the rectitude of our intentions, do, in the Name, and by Authority of the good People of these Colonies, solemnly publish and declare, That these United Colonies are, and of Right ought to be Free

and <u>Independent States</u>; that they are Absolved from all Allegiance to the British Crown, and that all political connection between them and the <u>State of Great Britain</u>, is and ought to be totally dissolved;... "[19] *(emphasis mine)*

We need to pause here for a moment to absorb what we have just read.

The Declaration of Independence asserts that the colonies, by Right, are now "Free and Independent States." But that is not the definition of "State" according to today's popular usage. We know there is a definite distinction between what we currently think and what our framers thought because in the very next clause, the Declaration refers to Great Britain as a "State." In our framer's mind, that word "State" was synonymous with Great Britain; it was synonymous with a sovereign government. Therefore in the minds of the framers, the minute they agreed to the Lee Resolution on July 2, 1776 and subsequently when their actions were published in the Declaration of Independence, **our Colonies became SOVEREIGN governments just like Great Britain, France, and Spain**. It is also important to note there was still *no mention of a central government.*

Reading further in the Declaration of Independence, we can see even more evidence of the sovereign nature of these newly independent States. The Declaration continues:

"and that as Free and Independent States, they have full Power to levy War, conclude Peace, contract Alliances, establish Commerce, and to do all other Acts and Things which Independent States may of right do."[20]

This Declaration not only equates each new State with Great Britain in title, but also in POWER, AUTHORITY, and RESPONSIBILITY. There is no legal difference in the minds of the signers of the Declaration of Independence between Great Britain and each newly independent and free State. It will be important for our later study to make note of the POWERS that belong to the States at the moment they became sovereign and independent.

*"as **Free and Independent States**, they have **full Power** to levy War, conclude Peace, contract Alliances, establish Commerce, and to **do all** other Acts and Things which Independent States may of right do."*[21] (emphasis added)

So the nature of the States is that they are sovereign, independent, and free governments that existed *prior to the establishment of a central government.* We will discover that the solution to controlling the federal government lies in the knowledge and application of the sovereignty of the States which they have possessed from the very founding of the Union.

Knowing the States existed prior to the federal government is also vital in understanding the nature of the Constitution and consequently, its proper application. The purpose of the Constitution, as the Preamble establishes, is to "Preserve the Blessings of Liberty to ourselves and our posterity."[22] Essential to the preservation of Liberty was the forming of a confederation and a central government that would work on behalf of the States in foreign affairs.

According to the third step of the Lee Resolution, the States would need to immediately procure "the assistance of foreign powers" to aid in their efforts to gain independence. Those that ratified the Lee Resolution recognized that these newly formed States had neither the manpower nor the resources to defeat Great Britain. Remember, the revolutionary war happened *after* the Declaration of Independence. Foreign aid and assistance would be necessary for Britain's inevitable and predictable response to the Declaration.

Also asserted within that third step, in addition to gaining foreign assistance, was an immediate necessity to form a confederation. The confederation was necessary not only in the beginning to ensure the success of the war for independence, but also to maintain their sovereignty after the coming war. As newly established sovereign entities that were cut off from the patronage of Great Britain, they were ill-prepared to take on the largest power in the world.

But going into debt to foreign nations and inviting foreign troops on your soil is rife with its own problems. With a confederation, they would be able to work together to pay off the debt to these foreign countries.

Having a union also provided the States with a unity that gave them safety in numbers. When the battle was over, this unity of the States can now make sure that the foreign troops that occupied their soil to aid in their independence from Great Britain would now politely go home. Without this bond between the States, they were in danger of being consumed by the very foreign countries that helped them gain their independence. It would be naïve to believe that France, Spain, and Holland were helping the Colonists from a purely philanthropic motivation and the founders knew this. Rest assured, these countries were looking for some benefit from their efforts. Territory in the New Land would be a great reward. If they could get land already colonized...BONUS.

The newly formed States had to ensure their sacrifice for independence was not in vain, not trading one foreign overlord for another. Uniting in a **confederation** (not a consolidation) was a very logical and effective way to protect that for which they had sacrificed - Life, Fortune, and Sacred Honor.

The long term solution for the preservation of Liberty was to create a central government. Its purpose would be to do as a single voice what the States would otherwise have to do individually. As Madison said, the central government would take care of "external objects...war, peace, negotiations, and foreign commerce."[23] Forming a Union would have been completely worthless if in order to trade or negotiate with foreign nations each State had to work independently. What if each foreign nation wanting to trade with the Union had to make thirteen separate treaties, with thirteen different rules, and thirteen different currencies? There would be no purpose for a Union. The Union allowed the colonies to do with one treaty something that would have had to have been done with thirteen. This would fulfill one of the greatest purposes our framers had in mind when declaring independence...for America to be the business hub of the world, not the world's policeman or nanny! The intent of the federal government was to act in the States' interest to protect and promote Liberty and prosperity within our borders.

In fact, listen to probably our greatest President's view on America's role on the world stage. It is certainly not a picture of a menacing, tyrannical behemoth. Hear George Washington in his Farewell Address share his vision for America.

Contrary to modern propaganda, Washington envisioned a federal government which was to be restrained not only domestically but even on the global scene. He says we must be fair and impartial in our dealing and not be blinded by so-called "alliances."

"Excessive partiality for one foreign nation and excessive dislike of another cause those whom they actuate to see danger only on one side, and serve to veil and even second the arts of influence on the other...The great rule of conduct for us in regard to foreign nations is in extending our commercial relations, to have with them as little

political connection as possible. So far as we have already formed engagements, let them be fulfilled with perfect good faith. Here let us stop.[24]

Thomas Jefferson in a letter to Elbridge Gerry, January 26, 1799 weighs in on this subject of foreign entanglement, as well:

"I am for free commerce with all nations; political connection with none; & little or no diplomatic establishment. And I am not for linking ourselves by new treaties with the quarrels of Europe; entering that field of slaughter to preserve their balance, or joining in the confederacy of kings to war against the principles of liberty."[25]

Further in Washington's farewell address, the first president cautions that our interests are distinctly our own, we are not Europe! We should not meddle unnecessarily in far-off conflicts or try to model our nation on the nations of Europe.

"Europe has a set of primary interests which to us have none; or a very remote relation. Hence she must be engaged in frequent controversies, the causes of which are essentially foreign to our concerns. Hence, therefore, it must be unwise in us to implicate ourselves by artificial ties in the ordinary vicissitudes of her politics, or the ordinary combinations and collisions of her friendships or enmities.

Our detached and distant situation invites and enables us to pursue a different course. If we remain one people under an efficient government. the period is not far off when we may defy material injury from external annoyance; when we may take such an attitude as will cause the neutrality we may at any time resolve upon to be scrupulously respected; when belligerent nations, under the impossibility of making acquisitions upon us, will not lightly hazard the giving us provocation; when we may choose peace or war, as our interest, guided by justice, shall counsel.

Why forego the advantages of so peculiar a situation? Why quit our own to stand upon foreign ground? Why, by interweaving our destiny with that of any part of Europe, entangle our peace and prosperity in the toils of European ambition, rivalship, interest, humor or caprice?"

And finally, Washington makes it clear that it's all about fair and open markets, not corporate cronyism and foreign welfare.

"Harmony, liberal intercourse with all nations, are recommended by policy, humanity, and interest. But even our commercial policy should hold an equal and impartial hand; neither seeking nor granting exclusive favors or preferences; consulting the natural course of things; diffusing and diversifying by gentle means the streams of commerce, but forcing nothing; establishing (with powers so disposed, in order to give trade a stable course, to define the rights of our merchants, and to enable the government to support them) conventional rules of intercourse, the best that present circumstances and mutual opinion will permit, but temporary, and liable to be from time to time abandoned or varied, as experience and circumstances shall dictate; constantly keeping in view that it is folly in one nation to look for disinterested favors from another; that it must pay with a portion of its independence for whatever it may accept under that character; that, by such acceptance, it may place itself in the condition of having given equivalents for nominal favors, and yet of being reproached with ingratitude for not giving more.

There can be no greater error than to expect or calculate upon real favors from nation to nation. It is an illusion, which experience must cure, which a just pride ought to discard.[26]

Clearly Washington didn't envision an all-powerful, far-reaching government that was involved in every aspect of global affairs, much less in every aspect of our daily lives!

Creating a Union was essential, but the framers also recognized that they needed to make sure the central government remained limited and defined and kept to its mission both domestically and abroad. The Constitution would be the way to limit and define this central government and give a watchful people the tools to keep it in check.

It is important to remember at this point, prior to September 17, 1787 and the subsequent ratification of our current Constitution, the central government we now know did not exist. Prior to March 1, 1781 and the ratification of the Articles of Confederation, there was no central government at all…just thirteen independent, sovereign, and free States. Remember, States are not as we currently perceive them when we think of Virginia, Georgia or New York, but rather are comparable to Spain, France, and Great Britain.

The sovereign States ratified the Constitution on behalf of the people. **The federal government had no role in the creation or ratification of the Constitution.**

The States came first.

The States were and still are sovereign governments.

The federal government did not exist at the State's independence day.

These are essential and foundational truths. With these truths and this foundation, we can now move on and discuss the LEGAL Nature of our Constitution.

3. A Contractual Agreement

The Nature Of The Constitution:

A Contract Among The States

Oftentimes I have heard well-intentioned citizens say something like, "The Constitution is a contract between the people and the federal government." I've heard not so well intentioned citizens say something like, "The Constitution made the federal government supreme over the States and they just have to obey what the federal government says." Is this truly the case? Is the Constitution a contract between the people and the federal government? Would that then give the federal government standing to somehow renegotiate the terms of the contract? Is it even possible for the federal government to be sovereign OVER the States? Let's look at this from a legal perspective and set the record straight.

Legally speaking, our Constitution is a binding contract between the States alone (as representatives of the voice of the people of those States). Technically, because it is a contract between sovereign governments, it is called a "compact". But for our purposes there is no difference operationally between a compact and a contract. So for simplicity sake, we will use the term contract.

All contracts have what we call, "parties to the contract." The parties of a contract are those entities that have engaged in the negotiation process called, "the meeting of the minds." This meeting of the minds is where the parties of the contract discuss, debate, and determine the purpose, parameters, and powers to be assigned through the contractual agreement. Once those items are settled upon, the parties sign the contract in a show of agreement. This signing, i.e. ratification of the contract, creates a legally binding agreement between the parties. To maintain that agreement, the parties to the contract must maintain the integrity of their promises so the agreement is not breeched. A breech of the agreements within the contract can void the contract and sever the binding force of the contract, thus relieving the parties of their responsibility to keep their promises.

We established in the previous chapter that the States existed prior to the Constitution as independent, sovereign, and free governments. The States as sovereignties came together and formed an alliance to negotiate a contract (The Constitution). Once the Constitutional contract was ratified, the provisions within that agreement brought the central government to life. The successful negotiation of that contract **created** a limited and defined central government whose purpose was to represent the States in those external objects of foreign relations & perform only the duties listed (enumerated) in the Constitution. Prior to the ratification of the Constitution, the central government was just an idea.

Simply stated, **the States are the parties to the Constitutional contract that CREATED the central government**. The central government is a creation of the States. The central government was intended to be an agent FOR the States, not a ruler OVER them. It is KEY to understand that the federal government has no sovereignty of its own outside the powers delegated to it by the States. That the States are not to be slaves to their own creation is an undeniable fact in light of the historical record of our founding.

Read through each of the following quotations carefully. The words of our founders make it abundantly clear how they viewed the position of the States in relation to the central government which the States themselves created:

*"The State Legislatures will **jealously and closely watch** the operations of this government, and be able to **resist** with more effect every assumption of power, than any other power on earth can do; and the greatest **opponent** to a federal government admit the State Legislatures to be sure **guardians** of the people's liberty."*[27] *James Madison*

*"I am for preserving to the States the **powers not yielded by them** to the Union, and to the legislature of the Union its constitutional share in the division of powers; and I am not for transferring all the **powers of the States** to the General Government, and all those of that government to the executive branch."*[28] *George Washington*

*"That the several states who formed [the Constitution], being **sovereign and independent**, have the unquestionable right to judge of its infraction;"[29] Thomas Jefferson*

*"Each **state retains its sovereignty**, freedom, and independence , and every Power, Jurisdiction and Right, which is not by this confederation expressly delegated to the United States, in Congress assembled."[30] Articles of Confederation.*

*"...the **true (protective) barriers** of our liberty in this country are our State governments."[31] Thomas Jefferson*

*"It is important to strengthen the State governments; and as this cannot be done by any change in the Federal Constitution (for the preservation of that is all we need contend for), **it must be done by the States themselves**, erecting such **barriers at the constitutional line** as cannot be surmounted either by themselves or by the General Government. The only barrier in their power is a wise government. A weak one will lose ground in every contest."[32] Thomas Jefferson*

*"In short, the government of each state is, and is to be, **sovereign and supreme in all matters** that relate to each state only. It is to be subordinate barely in those matters that relate to the whole; and it will be their own faults if the several states suffer the federal sovereignty to interfere in things of their respective jurisdictions."[33] John Dickinson*

(emphasis mine in the above quotations)

Now that we have described the legal framework and we have seen the framers' intent in reference to the power of the States, we can finally understand why the most effective and powerful tool to control the federal government is the proper assertion of the States' sovereignty.

All the power to govern was first delegated by the people to the States. The States, realizing the benefit of having a unified international voice, then delegated a portion of their power to the central government. At each step, the extent of the power delegated is to be diminished the further that it is removed from its source. This relationship is made clear through the Declaration of Independence and Madison's explanation in Federalist 45.

Notice first, in the Declaration of Independence, the States receive delegated power **from the people**:

"government receives its just powers from the consent of the governed...and that as Free and Independent States, they have full Power to levy War, conclude Peace, contract Alliances, establish Commerce, and to do all other Acts and Things which Independent States may of right do."[34]

Madison explains that through the Constitution, the central government receives delegated power **from the States**:

"The powers delegated by the proposed Constitution to the federal government are few and defined. Those which remain in the State governments are numerous and indefinite... The former (meaning the federal powers) will be exercised principally on external objects, as war, peace, negotiation, and foreign commerce; with which the last the power of taxation will, for the most part, be connected."[35] *(parenthetical mine)*

This makes the distribution of power very clear. The States are the delegators and the central government the delegate. Now that we have the legal and historical facts in place, the 10th Amendment now should be perfectly clear in meaning and application.

10th Amendment

"The powers not delegated to the United States, nor prohibited by it to the States, remains with the States or the People."[36]

When the 10th Amendment says "powers delegated," that is not the same as "surrender" or "forfeit". Even though the States delegated a portion of their power to the central government, they never relinquished anything. It was merely a "defined" transfer of power to the central government to perform a function on behalf of the States. Let me illustrate this point:

What if you were the owner of a fast food restaurant? In your capacity as owner you have the power to hire employees to do a job for you. You have hired employees to make French fries and burgers. In that capacity, you have "delegated" your power to those employees to make these items. What happens if the employee empowered to make the fries shows up one day and refuses to make fries? Or perhaps this employee decides to make the fries the way he wants, ignoring your operating procedures. What are you to do? As the owner, are you powerless in the face of this errant and rogue employee? Of course not! When you hired that employee to make the fries you did not "surrender" your power. He didn't become *your* boss. You hired him to do a job for *you*. You delegated a power to him, a power he can retain only as long as he does the job they way YOU want it to be done.

Continuing with this scenario, what if the employee hired to make fries comes to work one day and refuses to make fries, but instead pushes the employee making burgers off the grill and starts making burgers instead? Does the fry-making employee have the power to change his job without your permission? Of course not! He is defying your limitation of his power and stealing the power that was delegated to the employee making burgers.

It is not up to the employee to "interpret" your directions. You, as the original possessor of the French Fry Power, are the only one who can rightfully determine the meaning and application of your directions. It is the fry guy's job to simply carry out your instructions according to his job description. Nothing more, nothing less. Now that your employee has failed to do the job you hired him to do, that power comes back to you to do the job yourself or hire someone else to do it for you. And as the owner you have a duty to prevent the employee hired to make fries from taking power from the burger employee. One last question: is it against the law for you to fire this employee? Must you sue him in court to get him to stop errantly using your power? Of course not!

This is exactly the position of the States. The States are the original possessors of the power, - this was declared in the Lee Resolution and then again in the Declaration of Independence:

"Resolved, That these United Colonies are, and of right ought to be, free and independent States, that they are absolved from all allegiance to the British Crown, and that all political connection between them and the State of Great Britain is, and ought to be, totally dissolved."[37]

"That these United Colonies are, and of Right ought to be Free and Independent States; that they are Absolved from all Allegiance to the British Crown, and that all political connection between them and the State of Great Britain, is and ought to be totally dissolved; and that as Free and Independent States, they have full Power to levy War, conclude Peace, contract Alliances, establish Commerce, and to do all other Acts and Things which Independent States may of right do."[38]

The newly independent States delegated certain aspects of their power to the central government. That didn't make the central government their boss!

"The powers delegated by the proposed Constitution to the federal government are few and defined... The [federal powers] will be exercised principally on external objects, as war, peace, negotiation, and foreign commerce..."[39] James Madison

What they did not delegate was never lost, and what they did not list/enumerate is simply NOT a power authorized for the federal government to use or possess.

"The powers not delegated to the United States by the Constitution, nor prohibited by it to the states, are reserved to the states respectively, or to the people."[40] James Madison

Once the central government fails to do the job delegated, or operates outside the States' limitation of its power and instructions, the States have the power and are duty-bound to take back that delegated power and do the job themselves or find someone else to do the job for them.

The States literally and legally have the authority to deny the central government of its power or even "fire" them. The central government as a creation of the Constitution IS NOT AND CANNOT BE A PARTY TO THE CONSTITUTION. Let me say that again so that you don't miss it: the central government IS...NOT...A...PARTY...TO...THE...CONTRACT, IT IS A **CREATION** OF THE CONTRACT. The central government as a creation of the Constitution is an employee of the States and once the boss has determined the employee has failed to meet the employment standards, that employee can be dismissed! To place the federal government in the role of supervisor over the States is an aberration. To do so makes the creation superior to the creator. It literally makes the central government not only superior to the States, but also superior to the Constitution and the people themselves. If that happens, we are no longer a Republic, but a Kingdom - the very form of government from which our framers declared independence!

4. Acting Like Sovereign States

The contract (The Constitution) is between the sovereign parties (the States) and the federal government is a **creation** of the contract and not a party. What do the States do when their creation acts outside the parameters of the contract by engaging in actions not authorized, such as passing unconstitutional laws and regulations?

The framers considered it an absolute absurdity to think that the federal government acting outside of the constitutional charter for even a moment could be considered legitimate and binding upon the sovereign States:

"No legislative act, therefore, contrary to the Constitution, can be valid. To deny this, would be to affirm, that the deputy is greater than his principal; that the servant is above his master; that the representatives of the people are superior to the people themselves; that men acting by virtue of powers, may do not only what their powers do not authorize, but what they forbid."[41] *Alexander Hamilton*

Listen to the man who is called "The Father of the Constitution,"

"[for] the federal government to enlarge its powers by forced construction of the constitutional charter which defines them…so as to destroy the meaning and effect of the particular enumeration…the obvious tendency and inevitable result… would be, to transform the present republican system of the United States into an **absolute***, or, at best, a mixed* **monarchy***."*[42] *James Madison*

Interposition

When the federal government steps outside of its boundaries, since legally speaking we are a Constitutional Republic and not a kingdom or a democracy, our remedy lies with the States reasserting their sovereignty and taking responsibility for the power originally delegated to them by the People. The States have an obligation to protect the People from an abuse of power by the central government. This is accomplished when the States step in between the central government and the People to maintain the limited power of the central government. This works just like the manager of the restaurant restricting the employees to their hired positions and duties. This action of stepping in between the central government's abuse of power and the People is called "interposition."

*"in the case of deliberate, palpable, and dangerous exercise of other powers not granted...**the states...have the right, and are in duty bound, to interpose**, ...for maintaining, within their respective limits, the authorities, rights, and liberties..."[43]* James Madison

Interposition, as Madison says, is the duty of the States to protect the People from tyranny. The power and duty of the States to act in this protective capacity is founded on the understanding that the States are sovereign over the central government. Think about it, the States were the original possessors of this power. If they are not sovereign, it would be impossible for the States to have created and ratified a contract that created and delegated power to the central government. If the States are not sovereign, the Constitution cannot legally exist and the central government cannot exist. The very existence of the central government relies upon the sovereignty of the States. **For the central government to deny the States their sovereignty is for the central government to nullify its own existence.** For the States to allow the central government to exert a ruling power over them is to declare the States themselves irrelevant and to eliminate the purpose of even having States. Thomas Paine points out the principle that for Washington DC to rule over the States defies even the Laws of Nature:

"Small islands not capable of protecting themselves, are the proper objects for kingdoms to take under their care; but there is something very absurd, in supposing a continent to be perpetually governed by an island. In no instance hath nature made the satellite larger than its primary planet,"[44]

Remember, Madison explains in Federalist 45 that the powers delegated to the federal government are few and defined. He even lists them as "war, peace, negotiations, and foreign commerce," he classifies them as "external objects" or foreign affairs. But Madison continues with his explanation of powers delegated:

"The powers reserved to the Several States will extend to all the objects which, in the ordinary course of affairs, concern the lives, liberties, and properties of the people, and the internal order, improvement and prosperity of the State."[45]

The use of the word "reserved" lets us know that these powers, the "everything else" powers, are vested in the States ALONE. Madison makes it clear that enumerated powers are delegated to the federal government, and *everything else* belongs to the States. There are no gaps in delegated power, no power floating around waiting for some governmental entity to assume them. Therefore, when the federal government assumes undelegated power, it has to steal that power from the States. Stolen power has no authority.

*"Whenever the general government assumes undelegated powers, **its acts are unauthoritative, void and of no force.**"[46] Thomas Jefferson* (emphasis mine)

Imagine if someone stole your car. The thief then attempts to assert a legal authority over your car, trying to sell it or legally give someone else permission to use it. That is absurd! A thief has no legal authority to sell your car or give someone else permission to use it. Do you have to sue the thief in court to reassert ownership of your car? Of course not! All you need to do is prove your rightful ownership, perhaps by providing the title deed to the car, and that car is returned to you. If the central government assumes a power not delegated by the States through the Constitution, the central government is stealing that power from the States. The States do not have to sue the central government to get their power back, they simply need to provide the title deed to the ownership of their power. **That title deed is the Constitution**.

"The powers not delegated to the United States by the Constitution, nor prohibited by it to the states, are reserved to the states respectively, or to the people."[47] (emphasis mine) 10th Amendment.

Stolen power is void and of no force. To allow stolen power to have legal authority has very serious consequences.

"for the federal government to enlarge its powers by forced construction of the constitutional charter which defines them...so as to destroy the meaning and effect of the particular enumeration...the obvious tendency and inevitable result... would be, to transform the present republican system of the United States into an absolute, or, at best, a mixed monarchy."[48] James Madison

"No legislative act, therefore, contrary to the Constitution, can be valid. To deny this, would be to affirm, that the deputy is greater than his principal; that the servant is above his master; that the representatives of the people are superior to the people themselves; that men acting by virtue of powers, may do not only what their powers do not authorize, but what they forbid."[49] Alexander Hamilton

The most powerful and effective solution to an out of control central government, is to be found in the duty of the States to deny the central government the authority to use stolen power. The States must tell the central government they are operating outside the employment parameters. They must call this unauthorized use of power what it really is...theft, and theft is illegal. The States must refuse to recognize this unlawful use of power and declare it null and void. The States must refuse to comply and refuse to allow the federal government to enforce the stolen power. Many, including our founders, referred to this non-recognition of unconstitutional directives as *nullification.*

There are four common arguments against the States' rightful authority and duty to resist. States will get pushback from those who would like to see the central government usurp the sovereignty of the States. Each argument can be discounted thru legal, logical, and historical application of truth.

Argument #1: The States do not have the right to deny the federal government's assertion of power because it is not expressly in the Constitution to do so.

This argument fails on many levels. First, the right to control government of all forms lies in the hand of the People; *"government receives its just powers from the consent of the governed."*[50] Protecting our Liberty from unlawful government control is a **Natural Right**.

"Among the Natural Rights of the Colonists are these, First Life, secondly Liberty, third property, together with the Right to protect and defend them in the best means possible."[51] *Samuel Adams*

It is a Natural Right to have the authority to protect Life, Liberty, and Property. Government doesn't give you those rights; you possess them by the nature of your very existence. The 9th Amendment clearly recognizes all Rights in existence belong to the people, whether they are written down or not.

*"The enumeration in the Constitution, of certain rights, shall not be construed to deny or disparage others **retained by the people.**"[52] 9th Amendment* (emphasis mine)

The government has no power over the Rights of the People, expressed or not, unless the People expressly delegate them. The People, through the 10th Amendment, have indicated that powers are delegated in a limited form to the central government and in a broader form to the States, reminding that all the Power remains with the People. States are sovereign, as established in the Lee Resolution and subsequently declared through the Declaration of Independence. The central government has no power outside what the States and the People have delegated to it. Therefore, the States not only have the right but are duty bound to fulfil the purpose of the Constitution. The purpose of the Constitution, as expressed in the preamble, is to *"Preserve the Blessings of Liberty to ourselves and our Posterity."[53]* The States MUST do this or they have failed in the primary function of their Constitutional contract. If the States do not have power over the central government, then the Constitution has no authority. If the States, who created the Constitution, have no authority to enforce or maintain it, there remains no control over the central government. **What remains is a central government that is not limited by anything but its own will.** That is not a Republic; that is a Kingdom.

If all we have is a glorified Kingdom, then WE ARE NOT FREEMEN, but subjects to the central government. That is not what our framers fought for.

"Among the natural rights of the Colonists are these: First, a right to life; Secondly, to liberty; Thirdly, to property; together with the right to support and defend them in the best manner they can."[54] *Samuel Adams*

"...because the state legislatures will jealously and closely watch the operations of this government, and be able to **resist with more effect** *every assumption of power* **than any other power on earth can do***; and the greatest opponents to a federal government admit the state legislatures to be sure guardians of the people's liberty."*[55] *James Madison*

"the opposite doctrine which denies to the States the right of protecting their reserved powers, and which would vest in the General Government (it matters not through which department) the right of determining, exclusively and finally, the powers delegated to it, is **incompatible with the sovereignty of the States***, and of the Constitution itself, considered as the basis of the Federal Union."*[56] *John Calhoun*

Argument #2: The Supreme Court has already determined that the States do not have the power to deny the federal government the authority of usurped power.

This is one of the more absurd arguments. This argument attributes to the Supreme Court the power to determine the central government's boundaries and suggests that it is a ruling authority over the States. This argument fails legally, factually, and logically.

When the States created the central government, through the Constitution, they created three distinct branches; Legislative, Executive, and Judicial. All branches were created by the States and only exist because of the contract - The Constitution. But, if we allow the Judicial branch to determine the rightful powers of the central government, what we have done is allow the central government, through one of **its own branches**, to determine the limits of **its own power!**

If that happens, then the Constitution and the creators of that Constitution are not the limiting factors of the central government. The central government becomes the limit of its own power!

Let me be clear, The Supreme Court of the United States is PART of the central government. How can the central government determine the limits of its own power?

*"However true, therefore, it may be, that the judicial department, is, in all questions submitted to it by the forms of the Constitution, to decide in the last resort, this resort must necessarily be deemed the last in relation to the authorities of the other departments of the government; not in relation to the rights of the **parties** to the constitutional compact, from which the judicial as well as the other departments hold their delegated trusts. **On any other hypothesis, the delegation of judicial power would annul the authority delegating it;** and the concurrence of this*

department with the others in usurped powers, might subvert forever, and beyond the possible reach of any rightful remedy, the very Constitution which all were instituted to preserve."[57] James Madison

When the government is the sole determinant of its own power, two very destructive things happen. First, the States are no longer sovereign. The central government now becomes superior to the States. As Madison rightfully declares, to place the SCOTUS in the position of determining the extent of federal power is to nullify the power of the States and of the Constitution itself. It destroys the very nature of the Republic and fundamentally transforms America into a kingdom ruled by 9 black-robed co-regents, an oligarchy of thieves who have stolen power from the States and the people.

Pay careful attention to the following warnings:

"If the decision of the judiciary be raised above the authority of the sovereign parties to the Constitution... dangerous powers, not delegated, may not only be usurped and executed by the other departments, but that the judicial department, also, may exercise or sanction dangerous powers beyond the grant of the Constitution... consequently, that the ultimate right of the parties to the Constitution, to judge whether the compact has been dangerously violated, must extend to violations by one delegated authority as well as by another-- by the judiciary as well as by the executive, or the legislature"[58] James Madison

*"...we may fairly conclude, we are more in **danger** of sowing the seeds of arbitrary government in this department [referring to the Judicial Department] than in any other."[59] Thomas Jefferson*

"The great object of my fear is the federal judiciary. That body, like gravity, ever acting, with noiseless foot, and unalarming advance, gaining ground step by step, and holding what it gains, is ingulfing insidiously the special governments into the jaws of that which feeds them."[60] Federal Farmer

Secondly, if this is allowed then the Constitution <u>does not limit</u> the central government. The Constitution becomes impotent and irrelevant. The only limitation on central power is the federal government's own will.

*"That they will view this as **seizing the rights of the States**, and consolidating them in the hands of the general government, with a power assumed to bind the States, not merely in cases made federal, but in all cases whatsoever...that this would be to surrender the form of government we have chosen, and live under one **deriving its powers from its own will**, and not from our authority..."[61] Thomas Jefferson*

That is not a Republic, that is a Kingdom, an oligarchy!

*"It has long, however, been my opinion, and I have never shrunk from its expression,...that the germ of dissolution of our federal government is in the constitution of the federal judiciary ; **an irresponsible body**, (for impeachment is scarcely a scare-crow,) working like gravity by night and by day, gaining a little to-day and a little to-morrow, and advancing its noiseless step like a thief, over the field of jurisdiction, until **all shall be usurped from the States**, and*

the government of all be consolidated into one. To this I am opposed; because, when all government, domestic and foreign, in little as in great things, shall be drawn to Washington as the centre of all power, it will render powerless the checks provided of one government on another, and will become as venal and oppressive as the government from which we separated.[62] *Thomas Jefferson*

Argument #3: The Supremacy Clause establishes **all** federal law to be supreme over the States.

This simply cannot logically be so and the Supremacy Clause does not support this assertion. The Supremacy Clause reads:

"The Constitution, and the laws of the United States made in pursuance thereof…are the supreme law of the land."[63]

A simple and logical reading of this clause makes it clear that not all laws created by the central government are the supreme law of the land; only those made "in pursuance thereof." Laws made by congress (and Executive Orders issued by the president!) are only part of the laws enforceable on the people and the States if they are made in compliance with the Constitution. The central government cannot be the ones to determine their own compliance. That would be like having a criminal in the courtroom and the judge then asking the *criminal* to determine *his own* guilt or innocence!

The power to determine compliance with the Constitutional contract must remain with the creators of that contract; The States.

"the doctrine which denies to the States the right of protecting their reserved powers, and which would vest in the General Government (it matters not through which department) the right of determining, exclusively and finally, the powers delegated to it, is **incompatible with the sovereignty of the States**, *and of the Constitution itself, considered as the basis of the Federal Union."[64]* John Calhoun (emphasis mine)

The Supremacy Clause is very clear that <u>only laws made in compliance with the Constitution are valid</u>. Hamilton also states very clearly WHY this is important.

"No legislative act, therefore, **contrary to the Constitution**, *can be valid. To deny this, would be to affirm, that the deputy is greater than his principal; that the servant is above his master; that the representatives of the people are superior to the people themselves; that men acting by virtue of powers,* **may do not only what their powers do not authorize, but what they forbid."[65]** *Alexander Hamilton* (emphasis mine)

If we allow the central government to create any law, and then determine on their own whether that law is lawful or not, we declare the Constitution dead and the States irrelevant. The question our framers are posing to us, through this logical, factual, and legal truth, is simple; do you want to be a Republic where the People rule the government or do you want to be a Kingdom where the central government rules the People?

Argument #4: Giving the States the power to determine the application of federal law will allow the States to deny *any* law they don't like and we will devolve into anarchy.

This is not a lawful conclusion. The States have entered into a legally binding agreement with one another. In that legally binding contract, they have agreed to delegate certain powers to the central government. If the central government is acting within those proscribed limits, the States have no legal authority to deny that power. To do so would be to violate the contractual agreement with their partners, the other States. At which point the other parties to that contract could bring a grievance against the State in violation of the Contract. It is the States who would, as parties to the Contract, have proper legal standing to bring this legal grievance. The federal government is NOT a party to the contract, so it has NO standing to bring a grievance against the States. This proper application of law puts the courts in its proper role; deciding matters between the States.

"In all cases affecting ambassadors, other public ministers and consuls, and those in which a state shall be party, the Supreme Court shall have original jurisdiction. In all the other cases before mentioned, the Supreme Court shall have appellate jurisdiction, both as to law and fact, with such exceptions, and under such regulations as the Congress shall make."[66] Art. 3 sec. 2. cl. 2

The Supreme Court is NOT authorized to handle arguments of the federal government's own usurpation of power.

"However true, therefore, it may be, that the judicial department, is, in all questions submitted to it by the forms of the Constitution, to decide in the last resort, this resort must necessarily be deemed the last in relation to the authorities of the other departments of the government; **not in relation to the rights of the parties to the constitutional compact,** *from which the judicial as well as the other departments hold their delegated trusts."[67]* James Madison

But it can handle cases classified as "those in which a State shall be party."

So if the States wanted to enforce the Constitutional contract upon another State violating that promise, one could easily assert that Article III gives the Supreme Court that jurisdiction. This standing exists ONLY because the States are the parties to the Constitutional contract. The federal government is not a party to this contract and has NO STANDING to enforce it upon a State. Article III gives the Supreme Court no opportunity to define its own power. (See Prinz, Mack v. US, page 67 this book).

James Madison also explains the principle that States cannot arbitrarily decide which laws to follow and not follow, and cannot bind their nullification on other States.

*"But it follows, from no view of the subject, that a nullification of a law of the U. S. can **as is now contended**, belong rightfully to a single State, as one of the parties to the Constitution; the State not ceasing to avow its adherence to the Constitution. A plainer contradiction in terms, or a more fatal inlet to anarchy, cannot be imagined."[68] [Emphasis added]*

Madison is referring to a corrupted and distorted version of nullification which South Carolina's advocates proposed at that time. South Carolina was claiming that if one State nullified a federal act, it was void within that State and it could not be legally enforced until 3/4 of the other States overruled the nullification. What South Carolina was trying to assert was that a single State could control the entire country. Madison explained that is not what nullification is all about.

Ironically, many use this argument by Madison to deny the authority of the States to resist federal usurpations of power. Using Madison's statements in this way does two very obvious things. First, it takes Madison's comments out of the context in which they are used. Madison was never speaking against the authority of the States to deny *unlawful* use of power. For Madison to do that, we must accept the second obvious conclusion; Madison was either confused or a liar. Madison made it very clear that he believed not only that the States had the right, but were "duty bound" to deny unlawful use of federal power. In that same argument Madison DEFENDS nullification:

*"Thus the right of nullification meant by Mr. Jefferson is **the natural right, which all admit to be a remedy against insupportable oppression.** It cannot be supposed for a moment that Mr. Jefferson would not revolt at the doctrine of South Carolina, that a single state could constitutionally resist a law of the Union while remaining within it, and that with the accession of a small minority of the others, overrule the will of a great majority of the whole, & constitutionally annul the law everywhere."[69] [Emphasis added]*

Madison also firmly asserts that to allow the central government to assume powers not delegated would be dangerous and would change America from a Republic to a Monarchy.

*"for the federal government to enlarge its powers by forced construction of the constitutional charter which defines them…so as to destroy the meaning and effect of the particular enumeration…the obvious tendency and inevitable result… would be, **to transform the present republican system of the United States into an absolute, or, at best, a mixed monarchy.**"[70]*

When such a contradiction exists in one person's position, the logical conclusion is not to believe one position over the other, but to understand that there is NO CONFLICT, but only a misunderstanding in intent. Understanding the context in which Madison made both arguments is key to knowing that Madison was not confused and was not lying. He was simply pointing out that legally and factually the States, as the sovereign parties to the Constitution, have the power to govern the limitations created by the contract,

AND the States, who are parties to the contract have an obligation to accept the terms of the contract when they are legally applied. Additionally, the States cannot control the entire Union in a rogue effort to control the law.

Therefore, the argument of anarchy arising from the States randomly refusing to follow valid law fails, because once again, the States retain their sovereignty to pursue actions against States who fail to abide by their legally binding agreement. And the States retain their sovereignty from each other in the enforcement of a single State's actions.

In summary, the States being sovereign and independent parties to the constitutional contract, have the sole authority to determine the violations of that contract. This applies to violations by the federal government as well as by each other.

The federal government has no legal authority to assume powers not delegated.

The federal government has no authority to define its own power or limitations.

The People have entrusted that authority to the creators of the federal government; the States.

The number one solution to the out of control federal government problem rests with the sovereignty of the States. But the **existence** of sovereignty means absolutely nothing without the **exercise** of that sovereignty. How do the States exercise their sovereignty? By putting the federal government on notice that the proper authority is the Constitution and as creators of the Constitution, they are holding the federal government to those limitations. No authority beyond those specifically delegated will be recognized. As Kansas Secretary of State, Kris Kobach said in a speech regarding Eric Holder's denial of Kansas preservation of the Second Amendment, "The People of Kansas have spoken."[71]

But even those words are mere rhetoric if the States do not intend to stand by their word when the federal government tests their resolve. In the previous example, Kansas created a law that promised to criminally prosecute any federal officer that does not submit to the States authority and attempts to enforce unconstitutional federal gun laws. Kansas must be willing to do that, else their assertion of sovereignty is nothing more than bark with no bite. In the next chapter we will talk about a local solution to protect State sovereignty, some bite that stands behind the bark. Let's learn about the Constitutional Sheriff.

5. A New Sheriff In Town

One of the most critically important areas in our sovereign duty to protect American's Liberty is the Constitutional Sheriff and Peace Officer. Today with the tyranny of an ever-expanding federal government and the erosion of Liberty's protections, citizens are often threatened in their very homes and neighborhoods. Massive militarization of local law enforcement and a continual disregard for individual rights often brings fatal results. It is more important than ever to have constitutionally minded peace officers patrolling our streets. A Constitutional Sheriff can intercede when federal forces burst through their constitutional barriers. A Constitutional Sheriff can ensure that his officers have an informed and healthy regard for the principles they took an oath to uphold.

Historical Roots of the Sheriff

The Peoples' expectation for their Sheriff has changed somewhat over the centuries. The Anglo-Saxons divided their land into provinces, called Shyres. King Alfred the Great, who ruled from 849-899, allowed the Counts of the Shires to appoint deputies to administrate justice within the Shyres. The deputies were called "reeves". It is from this time that we get the word Shyrereeve, or Sheriff as we know today. The Reeve was considered the representative of royal authority in a shyre, with the highest authority as the senior official under the Crown. In the early 11th century, Great Britain would begin to use the Shyrereeves for the detection and prevention of crimes.

In early days, the Shyrereeve provided the castles with ammunition and other provisions, and they stocked and improved the king's manors; in short, the sheriff was the king's farmer, or bailiff, and the collector of all his rents and revenues within his district. His duty was then, as it still is, to support the justice of his county, and to keep the public peace.

The Shyrereeve was the first man in the county, and superior in rank to any nobleman. The Shyrereeve also heard and determined all causes, not exceeding forty shillings value, in the county court, and he had also a judicial power in several other civil cases. He executed writs and processes, proclaimed statutes, returned juries, and made return of writs for electing knights of the shire. Women as well as men, were appointed to the office of Shyrereeve, as well as several archbishops and bishops.

Although in the latter years of the reign of Edward I, the people elected their Sheriffs, for the most part Sheriffs were appointed by the King. Today the local sheriff is elected by the people of his county. He is the highest local Constitutional officer. He or she is not a bureaucratic appointee and does not represent the federal government. He is a representative of the People. The people are the boss of the Sheriff. His duty is to protect the rights of the people from all unlawful acts; even when those unlawful acts are by the government itself! If the Sheriff allows criminal acts to be perpetrated on the people, he is derelict in his duty.

The Sheriff takes an oath to support and defend the Constitution of the United States. (The Legislators of Virginia in 1799 called this oath a **duty**.) In that oath he is a representative of our rights. Samuel Adams said, *"Among the Natural Rights of the colonists are these…"[72]* Our founders were very clear what they believed our rights to be and where they came from. It should be very clear what the duty of the Sheriff ought to be. First and foremost his duty is to protect and defend the Constitutionally protected rights of his citizens.

We expect that our Sheriff, as much as he is able, will help to protect our homes, our property, our lives, and our families from the acts of those who would violate our rights. But what happens when it's the government itself who takes up the role of one who would take our rights, the role of the criminal? Is the Sheriff bound to uphold the law even when that law violates his oath to the Constitution and seeks to deprive the citizens their Liberty? Of course not! The duty and the obligations of the Sheriff do not change even when the violator of our Liberty is the government itself. To fail to protect our Liberty from all unlawful activity is a dereliction of duty.

The Constitution is the Supreme Law of the Land and it recognizes that "all men are created equal and endowed by their Creator with certain unalienable rights." Those rights retained, according to the 9th Amendment, are indefinite! But the powers delegated to the government, according to the 10th Amendment, are enumerated and defined. At no time is the government authorized to step outside of that limited box and infringe upon the unlimited rights of the people. The Sheriff, who is selected by the people, is charged with protecting and defending the Liberty of the people. But there are some things about the Sheriff we have forgotten. Let me ask a few questions to help illustrate just who your Sherriff really is.

Who is more powerful in your county, the Sheriff or the county commissioner? Remember the Sheriff is not hired by, nor is he required to take orders from your local government.

Who is more powerful in your county, the Sheriff or your State Legislator? Again, we must remember that the Sheriff is NOT hired by nor does he take orders from the State. If a State legislator breaks the law in the Sheriff's jurisdiction he goes to the hoosegow like anyone else.

Who is more powerful in your county, the Sheriff or your federal senator? If the State doesn't issue orders for our Sheriffs, the feds certainly do not. Remember the States are sovereign apart from the federal government.

Who is more powerful in your county, the Sheriff or the President of the United States? Did you know that the President cannot issue any executive order that is constitutionally or legally binding upon your Sheriff? But if the president comes to your county and commits a crime, the Sheriff can arrest the president and he doesn't have to ask anyone's permission to do so.

Our framers new that an essential check and balance on government power existed in limiting the sphere of federal power. Madison said;

"Hence a double security arises to the rights of the people. The different government will control each other, at the same time that each will be controlled by itself..."[3]

"The local or municipal authorities form distinct and independent portions of the supremacy, no more subject within their respective authorities than the general authority is subject to them, within its own sphere."[4]

Madison is saying that, yes, the federal government has authority, but that only exists within their sphere of delegated power. When they operate lawfully, they have supremacy. But that same supremacy exists in the local governments where they act within their delegated power. It just so happens that the powers delegated to the federal government are few and enumerated and the powers that remain locally are numerous and indefinite. When the federal government steps outside their sphere, their power is lost. The Sheriff is the local protector of the peoples' rights and in his sphere he or she is superior to all persons acting contrary to the rights of the people...including the government itself.

Sheriff Richard Mack

There is a revival taking place in America in the realm of Constitutional Sheriff, thanks in no small part to my good friend and probably the greatest champion for the cause, Sheriff Richard Mack. Sheriff Mack is the leader of the Constitutional Sheriffs and Peace Officers Association (CSPOA)[75] and won a landmark case at the Supreme Court in *Prinz, Mack v. U.S.* which affirmed the sovereignty of America's Sheriffs. Sheriff Mack could certainly tell his story better than I can, and I recommend that you get a copy of his book, *"The Constitutional Sheriff, America's Best Hope."*

Essentially, Sherriff Mack and Sheriff Prinz were two of a handful of peace officers courageous enough to take on the Clinton administration and live to tell about it. Under the infamous Brady laws, Sheriff's departments were being co-opted by the federal government to institute unconstitutional gun laws. Sheriff Mack did some soul-searching and decided that he had a duty before God to resist this tyranny. He swore an oath and his word meant something.

After a long fight all the way to the Supreme Court, Sheriff Mack and the Constitution prevailed. In the ruling the Justices declared that portions of the Brady bill were unconstitutional and that the federal government could not commandeer State or county officers to do its bidding. This case was a win not only for our Sheriffs but for the reassertion of Ninth and Tenth amendment principles.

Sheriff Mack now travels the country organizing and equipping Sheriffs to defend the citizens and honor their oath, and helping support and encourage those who are taking a stand. It is not easy to face down the feds. It takes guts. It takes character. It takes faith and tenacity. Sheriff Mack is doing his best to stir up these qualities in our Sheriffs, while delivering to them the knowledge they need to take a stand. I have had the honor of teaching with Sheriff Mack at numerous conventions. I have met hundreds of sheriffs and peace officers willing to take a stand. Let me mention just a couple.

Sheriff Nicholas Finch

A Sheriff that I had the pleasure of working with in his fight for *our* Liberty is Nicholas Finch and he is the Sheriff of Liberty County, Florida. Nick Finch was arrested by Governor Rick Scott's Department of Law Enforcement for standing in defense of the Constitution and honoring his oath of office. What was Finch's crime? He refused to pursue the prosecution of a man who was arrested for simply possessing a firearm.

"A well regulated militia, being necessary to the security of a free State, the right of the people to keep and bear arms shall not be infringed."[76]

You see, Sheriff Finch believes the Second Amendment means what it says, our Right to keep and bear arms SHALL NOT BE INFRINGED. He made the decision not to pursue a charge against Floyd Parish after he was detained for possessing a firearm without a conceal and carry permit. Did Sheriff Finch break the law? On the contrary, what Sheriff Finch did was well within his authority and in full compliance with recordkeeping rules and regulations in Florida. More importantly, Sheriff Finch was standing true to his oath to support and defend the Constitution. What Sheriff Finch did was stand in the gap where the government is trying to erode your Liberty. Here's the short version.

Mr. Parish was driving in the forest near his home and had a small pistol in his pocket that he used to signal his wife in case his chronic health issues got him into trouble as he worked on their property. When a deputy pulled him over in the forest, he saw the pistol and detained him for possession of a firearm (a constitutionally protected right) and took him to the local jail. Upon assessing the situation and consulting with a judge for good measure, Sheriff Finch removed Parish's file from the records and removed his name from the jail log. Well within his authority; *The General Records Schedule for Law Enforcement, Correctional Facilities, and District Medical Examiners* outlines this authority.

ARREST RECORDS: OFFENDER INFORMATION
Item #32

This record series documents each adult and juvenile arrested. The records provide such information as complete name; alias or nickname; residence; sex; age; date of birth; place of birth; height; weight; color of hair; color of eyes; complexion; race; date of arrest and/or offense; offense committed; car make, year, license number, and state; occupation; habits; name of closest relative or friends; scars, marks, or tattoos; any abnormalities; and special remarks. The juvenile records may also include parent(s) or guardian's name(s), telephone number(s), and occupation(s). If the arrest results in an investigation, the record should be filed with the applicable Criminal Investigative Records item. See also "CRIMINAL INVESTIGATIVE RECORDS" items, "CRIMINAL HISTORY SUMMARY RECORDS/RAP SHEETS," and "MASTER NAME INDEXES."

RETENTION:

a) Record copy. Retain until obsolete, superseded, or administrative value is lost.

b) Duplicates. Retain until obsolete, superseded, or administrative value is lost.[77]

When Sheriff Finch used his proper authority not to pursue charges against Mr. Parish, the records pertaining to his arrest lost their "administrative value." Sheriff Finch, by this Florida Regulation was within his authority to destroy this record.

The arrest affidavit of Sheriff Finch gives a pretty detailed account of what took place. But the arrest affidavit NEVER mentions Parish being booked into custody. Being placed in a jail cell is not being booked. If the arrest affidavit is accurate, and we have to trust it to be as it was given under oath, then Parish was never booked so the log that contained his name was in error and the Sheriff's office also had full authority to white out his name and make space for someone who was actually booked into the jail.

After releasing Mr. Parish, Sheriff Finch himself was arrested, relieved of his elected office by Florida Department of Law Enforcement and endured months without pay and was criminally prosecuted by Governor Rick Scott's close friend Willie Meggs. Sheriff Finch never broke a law and never even violated a regulation. So what was he being accused of doing?

The arrest affidavit claims Sheriff Finch violated Florida Statute 838.022(1). This statute reads:

"It is unlawful for a public servant, with corrupt intent to obtain a benefit for any person or to cause harm to another, to: (b): Conceal, cover up, destroy, mutilate, or alter any official record or official document or cause another person to perform such an act:..."[78]

Was Florida Governor Scott trying to say that when Sheriff Finch defended our Constitutionally protected Rights he was acting with "corrupt intent?" Have we really come to the point in our country where honoring your oath to "support and defend the Constitution" and wanting to "secure the Blessings of Liberty to ourselves and our posterity" is a crime of corrupt intent even in the eyes of our so-called conservative governors?

Is Governor Scott trying to tell us that when Sheriff Finch stood in defense of our Constitutionally protected Rights he was conferring upon Mr. Parish a "benefit." The Second Amendment is NOT a benefit, it is a protection against government assault on a God-given RIGHT. The last time I checked, it was called a Bill of Rights not a Bill of Benefits.

Do you think Sheriff Finch should have just shut up and enforced the law even knowing it is unconstitutional? I hope not. He took oath to support and defend the Constitution of the United States FIRST, not an oath to support and defend unconstitutional laws. If you believe officers should simply enforce all the laws regardless of their oath, then why in the world do they even take an oath? Is it just a pleasant formality that looks good in a ceremony or does it actually mean something? It is a man of honor who will stand for his word, even when it might be unpopular, even when it might hurt. Sheriff Finch appears to be such a man of honor. Some may remember an incident in our recent history where a Sheriff should have stood for what was right. Instead the Sheriff chose to simply enforce the law. On that day, Rosa Parks was arrested for refusing to sit in the back of the bus.

The Second Amendment clearly states our Right to keep and bear arms SHALL NOT BE INFRINGED! Sheriff Finch believes in the Constitution. He believes in his oath.

Sheriff Finch refused to give up his fight even when threatened by the State Attorney prosecuting him. He took this battle to a jury trial and the jury found him not guilty. It is interesting to note that the State Attorney's argument was so ridiculous and so obviously unfounded, that the judge had to stop the court proceedings to tell the audience to stop laughing at the prosecutor's absurd arguments.

Florida Governor Rick Scott was finally forced to reinstate Sheriff Finch, after having ignored the citizens' pleas to intervene while the Sheriff and his family were dragged through a torturous and unnecessary ordeal. Sheriff Finch did nothing wrong. He defended the Constitution. He stood in the gap for us. This is the proper role of the Sheriff. This is what a Constitutional Sheriff looks like.

Sheriff Brad Rogers

One more Constitutional Sheriff I want to mention is Sheriff Brad Rogers of Elkhart County, Indiana. Sheriff Rogers' experience illustrates the utter lawlessness and corruption that has overtaken our federal government.

The unconstitutional executive agency known as the Food and Drug Administration (FDA) has been waging a relentless war on the terrifying menace of …wait for it… RAW MILK! Under the pretense that tainted milk was traced to a raw milk producer in Michigan in 2007, the FDA commenced SWAT team raids on Amish milk farmers in Indiana in the dead of night. Raw milk famer, David Hochstetler was raided and harassed continually throughout 2010 and 2011. Finally, Sheriff Rogers had enough. After several confrontations, he sent a letter to the FDA informing them that if they stepped foot in his county again they would be arrested. As far as I know the farmer has not been bothered since. This may seem like a minor example (unless you are the farmer and his family) but it begs the question: What would your Sheriff do?

What About Your Sheriff?

Do you have a Sheriff that is so committed to Constitutional government and Liberty that he would protect your family from federal swat teams that have so little regard for freedom and human life that they would put your family at risk over raw milk? If he won't protect you from milk raids, can you depend on him to stand in the gap on even weightier matters? What if snipers show up because your livestock is trespassing, or you have been deemed a threat to turtles? What if DOE SWAT teams kicked down your door for unpaid tuition bills?

Would your Sheriff sit down with Rosa Parks or drag her off the bus? Would he or she say "I don't make the laws, I just enforce them?"

There is a way to know for sure if your Sheriff is a Constitutionally minded Sheriff or not. Go sit down and talk to him or her. Ask some very important questions. For example:

1. Will you require all federal agents to inform you and obtain your permission before serving warrants on your citizens?

2. Will you verify all warrants served by the federal agents are in full compliance with the 4th, 5th, and 6th Amendments?

3. Will you ensure all federal warrants are issued by a court of common law, not an Administrative Law court, and all warrants are complete with the following elements?

   a. Warrant is based upon probable cause;

   b. Warrant has oath verified by a common law court of local jurisdiction;

   c. Warrant has specifically listed the places to be searched; AND

   d. Warrant has specifically listed the persons or things to be seized?

(There are NO OTHER exceptions to your right to be free from unreasonable searches and seizures. The 4th Amendment makes no mention of "national security," "exigent circumstances," or "officer safety." These are all exceptions to YOUR rights created by the government. They are literally the government expanding its own power through the courts who are paid by the government.)

4. Will you ensure that all of your officers and staff are properly trained in the principles they took an oath to support and defend?

After these questions are answered, regardless of whether they are answered correctly, ask your Sheriff to sign the CSPOA Resolution affirming his compliance to the Constitution. (See the complete resolution in the Appendix B) You can print out a copy of this resolution by visiting CSPOA.org.[79]

Do not except excuses like, "I have to enforce the law." Your Sheriff's obligation and oath is to support and defend the Constitution – the Supreme Law of the Land. Your Sheriff's duty to preserve Liberty overrides any and all obligation "to enforce the law."

Make sure your Sheriff has a copy of Richard Mack's book *"The Constitutional Sheriff, America's Best Hope."* Will your Sheriff attend a Constitutional workshop held by CSPOA or KrisAnne Hall? If your Sheriff is not willing to pledge to defend the Constitution above the law; If your Sheriff is not willing to get educated on his Constitutional DUTY, then you do not have a Constitutionally-minded Sheriff. If you don't have a Constitutionally-minded Sheriff, then quite frankly, you and your family are not safe and your Liberty is not secure.

6. Article V Convention

"The Congress, whenever two thirds of both houses shall deem it necessary, shall propose amendments to this Constitution, or, on the application of the legislatures of two thirds of the several states, shall call a convention for proposing amendments, which, in either case, shall be valid to all intents and purposes, as part of this Constitution, when ratified by the legislatures of three fourths of the several states, or by conventions in three fourths thereof, as the one or the other mode of ratification may be proposed by the Congress..."[80] Article V, U.S. Constitution

Article V Convention is a structural fix aimed at making corrections at the federal level. It is a Constitutional remedy inserted into the Constitution to allow the people to provide for further protections within the federal framework. It is a legal way to amend the Constitution as we recognize threats to Liberty and seek to improve the safeguards of our republican system. Article V Convention aims to make structural changes or further clarifications to the operations of the federal government and its relation to the States. A convention seeks to fix what is assumed to be broken or lacking in the federal system. Since it involves an actual change to the Constitution itself, one could reasonably argue that it should be used only in the rarest of circumstances and is for that reason one of the most difficult to carry out.

Our framers anticipated the need to amend the Constitution as our awareness of Liberty expanded and perhaps our need for government diminished. Listen to

Thomas Jefferson's view on amending the Constitution. It appears clear that he felt it was needed, but not to be taken lightly:

"I am certainly not an advocate for frequent and untried changes in laws and constitutions. I think moderate imperfections had better be borne with; because, when once known, we accommodate ourselves to them, and find practical means of correcting their ill effects. But I know also, that laws and institutions must go hand in hand with the progress of the human mind. As that becomes more developed, more enlightened, as new discoveries are made, new truths disclosed, and manners and opinions change with the change of circumstances, institutions must advance also, and keep pace with the times. We might as well require a man to wear still the coat which fitted him when a boy, as civilized society to remain ever under the regimen of their barbarous ancestors."[81]

It is also interesting to note Jefferson's reliance on the "enlightenment" of the people to become more distant to the "barbarous ancestors," clearly implying that amendments should be for the expansion of Liberty and not for the further bondage of the people.

I'm quite sure our framers never intended for us to continually amend the Constitution to expand federal power or for light or transient reasons. If that had been the case, our framers would have allowed the federal government to freely amend the Constitution without a final check of the States and the people. They wouldn't have made the process so difficult to complete.

It is important to note that the provisions for amending the Constitution do not make the Constitution a "living, breathing, document." The "living, breathing, document" nomenclature has very little to do with formal and Constitutional means of amending the Constitution and everything to do with the reinterpretation of words OUTSIDE of the amendment process. This "living, breathing, document" classification is not only patently false, but insidiously dangerous as it allows the government and their courts to functionally amend the Constitution without submitting to the constitutional process. Historically, these "lexical amendments" have not been to advance Liberty but to expand government power. This fallacy of Constitutional interpretation proves the very need for a formal and arduous means of Constitutional Amendments. You cannot have a foundation that ever changing. You might as well attempt to build your house upon vanilla pudding. The Constitution is a foundational rock that can be added upon to expand the Liberty building. And a rock of this magnitude shall not be moved, or else the entire building will crumble.

There are numerous sources available discussing Article V convention. What does the Constitution say about Article V? What do the framers say about Article V? I recommend the *Journal of the Federal Convention Kept by James Madison (ed. by E.H. Scott; R. R. Donnelly & Sons Co., Chicago, 1893)* and The Founders' Constitution at <u>http://press-pubs.uchicago.edu/founders/</u> which contains many writings of the founders in digital form, including Madison's journal of the constitutional conventions.

Though I have never taken a stance in opposition to this constitutionally authorized remedy, I have been personally attacked and ridiculed for pointing out the fact that we must consider some inherent dangers and take measures to prepare for them. Many act as if Article V is a panacea to our current constitutional crisis and to consider that there may be difficulties is somehow seen as foolish. Contrary to those viewpoints, there was much debate in 1787 surrounding the proposals for amending the Constitution. The founders were not of one mind on this issue and many saw dangers in the proposal. For instance George Mason, Edmund Randolph and Elbridge Gerry were so concerned about a tyrannical Congress controlling the process that they refused to sign the Constitution that came out of the convention.

"Amendments therefore will be necessary, and it will be better to provide for them, in an easy, regular and Constitutional way than to trust to chance and violence. It would be improper to require the consent of the Natl. Legislature, because they may abuse their power, and refuse their consent on that very account." - George Mason, June 11, 1787[82]

In this present writing, I want to present for the reader's consideration some of the issues that concerned the founders, in particular the potential of a Congress that "may abuse their power."

Indeed there will undoubtedly be occasions where an Article V convention may be necessary. If we are going to have an Article V convention, we should want to know the CHALLENGES that we will have to overcome? And if there are indeed threats to the process, we need to deal with those threats honestly and openly rather than jump in feet first, eyes closed, and hope for the best. To use a metaphor shared with me by a 30-year attorney, surely warning your child not to "play in the streets" could not be considered foolish. I would view that as good parenting, even if a car never comes by.

Article V is like conducting open heart surgery on the Constitution. We should be fully informed of all the benefits AND RISKS before we enter into such a serious procedure. Patrick Henry said in 1775:

"...it is natural to man to indulge in the illusions of hope. We are apt to shut our eyes against a painful truth, and listen to the song of that siren till she transforms us into beasts. Is this the part of wise men, engaged in a great and arduous struggle for liberty? Are we disposed to be of the number of those who, having eyes, see not, and, having ears, hear not, the things which so nearly concern their temporal salvation? For my part, whatever anguish of spirit it may cost, I am willing to know the whole truth; to know the worst, and to provide for it."[83]

I want to know the truth, no matter how unpleasant or frightening it might be, so we can be prepared to deal with these difficult issues.

I want to bring forward several of the challenges that I see that must be addressed before we run headlong blindly into the most constitutionally invasive means of controlling the federal government -Article V Convention.

WHO are the delegates and what is their motivation?

In the convention debates of 1787, James Madison supported the idea of Congress proposing amendments but he expressed concern over a convention process as to *"How was a Convention to be formed? by what rule decide? what the force of its acts?"*[84]

Later in 1788 Madison reveals his biggest concern – Who will be the delegates and what will be their motivation?

"If a General Convention were to take place for the avowed and sole purpose of revising the Constitution, it would naturally consider itself as having a greater latitude than the Congress appointed to administer and support as well as to amend the system; it would consequently give greater agitation to the public mind; an election into it would be courted by the most violent partizans on both sides; it wd. probably consist of the most heterogeneous characters; would be the very focus of that flame which has already too much heated men of all parties; would no doubt contain individuals of insidious views, who under the mask of seeking alterations popular in some parts but inadmissible in other parts of the Union might have a dangerous opportunity of sapping the very foundations of the fabric. Under all these circumstances it seems scarcely to be presumeable that the deliberations of the body could be conducted in harmony, or terminate in the general good. Having witnessed the difficulties and dangers experienced by the

*first Convention which assembled under every propitious circumstance,
I should tremble for the result of a Second, meeting in the present
temper of America, and under all the disadvantages I have mentioned.*[85]

In Federalist 49 Madison discusses two options for
choosing delegates to a convention: either through the
Legislators or through popular vote of the people. In each
case he believed there was cause for concern. Those
concerns are all very relevant to us today. We must use this
wisdom to protect our Constitution from those who would
destroy it.

In modern terms, when delegates are chosen by the
legislators, what we could see are appointments based upon
party loyalty rather than upon Constitutional expertise and
dedication to sound Liberty principles. When the
delegates are chosen by popular vote, typical election
dynamics could determine the outcome. Voters would
vote based upon party popularity and perhaps even a
"lesser of two evils" and the same corrupt politicians would
now be "fixing" the very problems they created. The
ultimate result of both options would be, as Madison states,
*"The same influence which had gained them an election into the
legislature, would gain them a seat in the convention... They would
consequently be parties to the very question to be decided by them."*[86]

According to Madison, the real difficulty with delegates
boils down to "motivation." What will be the motivating
force behind the delegates and their amendments?
Madison recognized, and we should remember, that the

only reason we have our current Constitution is that the framers had just come from a bloody revolution which kept the delegates focused upon LIBERTY. It is this focus that forced them to set aside their party politics and personal motivations:

"We are to recollect that all the existing constitutions were formed in the midst of a danger which repressed the passions most unfriendly to order and concord; of an enthusiastic confidence of the people in their patriotic leaders, which stifled the ordinary diversity of opinions on great national questions; of a universal ardor for new and opposite forms, produced by a universal resentment and indignation against the antient government;"[87]

Madison is telling us that without some overriding and unifying motivation, the convention would likely degrade into a morass of factional passions, the same tired Republican vs. Democrat drama we see today. If we cannot get delegates that are properly constitutionally minded, rather than driven by political gain and greed, Article V will never serve the cause of true Liberty. Therefore, the selection of delegates is a very important aspect to consider.

A second question to ask is…

How Long Will It Take?

One big difference between the choices of nullification and Article V Convention is the time each takes to implement. Any advocate of Article V must admit that this is a LONG TERM goal and not a quick fix. To call a convention, choose delegates, and agree on amendments; an Article V convention could take a long time, maybe up to 5 to 10 years. Adding to the time frame is the Article V requirement of 3/4 ratification by the States. That means EVERY AMENDMENT must be agreed upon (debated, with amendments), individually, by 3/4 of the States to ratify.

When our country was born, only 13 colonies were involved and the total population in America was about 3 million. It took nearly 20 years of crisis to reach a boiling point in 1776. It then took from 1776 to 1790 (14 years) for the final State, Rhode Island to finally ratify the Constitution. That was not so much due to primitive means of communication as it was to debate and wrangling over various provisions and a battle for a Bill of Rights. Today we have 50 States and a population of almost 310 million! Some may ask do we even have that much time? If we do (or do not!), it would be prudent during that time to use nullification to put the brakes on at the State level until corrections (if truly needed) can be made at the federal level.

Here is the big question regarding Article V conventions…

What Does Congress Think An Article V Convention Should Look Like?

As noted above, several founders considered this a major issue with the Article V process. It would indeed be foolish (and rather arrogant) to dismiss the concerns of the very men who wrote the Constitution itself. There have been many discussions on what the Constitution says about Article V, what the framers say about Article V, but the REAL LIFE question is what Congress will actually DO if we call a convention.

The good news is we don't have to guess what Congress thinks about an Article V convention. On July 9, 2012, The Congressional Research Service (CRS), quite often the opinion factory of Congress, published a report titled, "The Article V Convention to Propose Constitutional Amendments: Contemporary Issues for Congress. In this document the CRS tells us what Congress thinks and has thought about Article V conventions since the 1950's.

Let us begin by reviewing the relevant sections of Article V:

"The Congress, whenever two thirds of both houses shall deem it necessary, shall propose amendments to this Constitution, or, on the application of the legislatures of two thirds of the several states, shall call a convention for proposing amendments, which, in either case, shall be valid to all intents and purposes, as part of this Constitution, when ratified by the legislatures of three fourths of the several states, or by conventions in three fourths thereof, as the one or the other mode of ratification may be proposed by the Congress..."[88]

The first thing we must point out is that the Article V provision is not a means of "bypassing" the Congress. Congress is very obviously part of the process. A "Convention of States" that proposes to operate on its own and "bypass" Congress is an unconstitutional and rogue process.

Clearly, Article V requires Congress, on the application of two thirds of the States, to "call" a convention for "proposing amendments." Once the convention is called, the proposed amendments must be ratified by three quarters of the States. Congress is authorized to choose what method of ratification in the States, by either ad hoc conventions called by the States for the specific purpose of considering ratification, OR ratification by the legislatures of the States. But this is a process and there are certain details in the procedure that are not mentioned in the text of the Constitution. Congress is more than willing to fill in those blanks. According to the CRS report, Congress has already altered the Article V process by inserting three additional elements NOT in Article V of the Constitution:

1. The Congressional vote to propose an amendment must be approved by two thirds vote of members present and voting, providing a quorum is present;

2. Amendments are not incorporated into the existing text of the Constitution as declared in 1788 but included as "supplementary articles"; and

3. Beginning in the 20th century, Congress has required that ratifications must be contemporaneous, meaning every amendment must be ratified within a seven year deadline.[89]

But what does Congress see as its key role in an Article V convention? The CRS points out that Congress believes that Article V delegates important and exclusive authority to Congress over the Article V Process. The CRS shows us the authority Congress claims Article V delegates to them:

1. The Right to propose amendments directly;

2. The Responsibility to "call" conventions; and

3. The Responsibility to submit proposed amendments to the States for ratification.[90]

The problem that exists is that the Constitution is silent on the mechanics of HOW Congress is to complete their three tasks. The CRS points out that Congress has traditionally laid claim to a broad spectrum of responsibilities. In addition to the three authorities listed above, the CRS lists six more which Congress declares that fall within their purview:

1. Receiving, Judging, and Recording State Applications;

2. Establishing procedures to summon a convention;

3. Setting a time allotted for deliberations;

4. Determining the number and selection of delegates;

5. Setting INTERNAL convention procedures; and

6. Arranging for formal transmission of proposed amendments to the States.[91]

Congress asserts that when considering all that needs to be done, they have an "indispensable and defining role"[92] in the Article V Convention process. A large part of that indispensable and defining role of Congress, as shown by the CRS through Congressional precedent, will be filling in those procedural blanks. There are many issues addressed in this thirty-two page report. We will, however, only deal with five major questions:

1. Is Congress obligated to call a convention?

2. What kind of convention will it be, a general or limited convention?

3. Does Congress have to submit all proposed amendments for ratification?

4. Who are the delegates and what is their motivation?

5. What role does the President play in an Article V Convention?

To fill in the blanks Congress will ask and amazingly, Congress will also *answer* these questions as well.

Must Congress Call a Convention?

First let's see if Congress believes it must call a convention or not. Article V says, "Congress SHALL call a convention..." (emphasis mine) Alexander Hamilton said in Federalist #85:

"By the fifth article of the plan, the Congress will be obliged "on the application of the legislatures of two thirds of the States [which at present amount to nine], to call a convention for proposing amendments, which shall be valid, to all intents and purposes, as part of the Constitution, when ratified by the legislatures of three fourths of the States, or by conventions in three fourths thereof." The words of this article are peremptory. The Congress "shall call a convention." Nothing in this particular is left to the discretion of that body. And of consequence, all the declamation about the disinclination to a change vanishes in air."[93]

All things considered, the directive seems very clear. However, things are never that clear when dealing with politicians and governments. The catch is Congress has given itself the authority to determine the validity of the States' applications. In determining the **validity** of the applications, they also set the standards for that validity. The CRS report instructs that Congress is able to declare a petition "defective" and therefore invalid.[94] Invalid applications cannot be used to call a convention. And we begin to see just how powerful Congress really can be.

So what does Congress consider a valid application to look like? The CRS says "most constitutional scholars" hold that "applications proposing a specifically worded amendment" are invalid.[95] Why? Because, these scholars claim, the purpose of the convention is not to ratify an amendment but to deliberate and propose amendments. To allow only specific amendments to be addressed in a convention would, according to these scholars, eliminate a vital step in the process of an Article V Convention. So, according to Congress if the State has an amendment for a specific purpose with specific wording, the State's application is invalid. Do you agree with this opinion?

Congress grants itself another power regarding State applications by declaring that applications must have an expiration date. If Congress declares the application too old, the States must resubmit.

Finally, Cyril Brickfield, counsel to the House Judiciary Committee from 1951-1961, told Congress they didn't really need to call a convention if they didn't want to, even if all the applications were received.

"...it is doubtful, however, that there is any process or machinery by which Congress should be compelled to perform this duty."[96]

Brickfield pointed out that in 1920 Congress was mandated by the Constitution to reapportion the House of Representatives, but did not and nothing happened. He claims this failure to act set a precedent that even if Congress fails to call a convention, even when thirty-four States properly petition, there really is *"no enforceable cause of action."*[97] By reminding Congress of Brickfield's advice, the CRS is prompting Congress, *"don't worry; there is no reason to call a convention if you don't want to because there is no recourse available to the States if you refuse."*

One could obviously argue that the States could sue Congress in federal court to force a convention. How long would that take? What guarantee would the States have that the courts would rule in their favor? After all, the Supreme Court has already upheld Congressional add ins to Article V. Aren't the federal courts filled with judges who are appointed by the federal government? Do we think there is a likelihood that they would rule in favor of the States and against its own interest? Is this a gamble worth taking?

According to Congress, the CRS report shows, the answer to the question, "Must Congress Call a Convention?" is a resounding "NO!" Yes, the Constitution demands it. Yes the founders said Congress was obligated. BUT Congress sets the standards for applications, so they can simply refuse applications to avoid a convention. And, according to the CRS, precedent has been set in the 1920's that says Congress can simply REFUSE and the States have no recourse.

I hope we are seeing a pattern here. I hope we can recognize that Congress feels Article V gives them a ruling authority and supremacy over the States. I hope we can listen and learn from Congress' own actions how they believe this Article V Convention will practically play out. As we can see by the very first question, the practical application of a convention has nothing to do with the Constitution and nothing to do with framer's intent. It is clear that, in fact, an unconstitutional mindset which has gripped Congress for years (isn't that the reason we are having this discussion?) could be a significant threat to the

Article V process, just as George Mason believed it would be!

"Col: Mason thought the plan of amending the Constitution exceptionable & dangerous. As the proposing of amendments is in both the modes to depend, in the first immediately, and in the second, ultimately, on Congress, no amendments of the proper kind would ever be obtained by the people, if the Government should become oppressive, as he verily believed would be the case." [98]

Remember that Congress has the responsibility of "calling" a convention upon application from two thirds of the States. We have already learned that Congress, even from a minimalistic perspective, has placed itself in a supervisory role over all Article V procedures. It was clear by the CRS report that Congress believes it not only receives petitions, but it also sets the criteria for legitimate petitions and then has the authority to determine whether those petitions meet Congressional standards and are valid. In this way, Congress can choose to call a convention or not, based upon acceptance or denial of the States' applications.

To understand Congress's next position, we will have to operate on the premise that a sufficient number of valid applications have been received and now Congress is going to decide what kind of convention there will be; a limited convention or a general convention. Just so there is no confusion, I am aware of what the Constitution says and what our framers say. But we must look closely at what Congress says so we can be prepared to deal with this reality if a convention is to be called. If someone said that they were coming to your house to punch you in the face, you would likely take reasonable actions to deal with the forthcoming events. Like get your Louisville slugger positioned close to the door! So, yes, I know what the founders believe. I know what I believe. What is germane to the present discussion is what **Congress** believes, or more importantly, what they have already declared that they will or can do in regards to a convention. Because we have *seen* what Congress believes and what the Constitution *requires* are rarely the same. Moving on...

It is important to remember certain conclusions that Congress has already drawn.

1. Congress is the controlling authority in determining the validity of applications, thus giving Congress a controlling supremacy over the States.

2. Congress has been advised by "experts" that applications that assert specifically worded amendments are invalid because the purpose of the convention is to *propose* amendments, not *ratify* them.

3. Congress has the power to choose to not call a convention if they don't want to, even with sufficient valid petitions, because precedent has been set in the 1920's that establishes there is no recourse available to the States for Congressional failure to act.

So to summarize, the federal government has deemed itself superior to the States *yet again* by defining the rules of the game.

Type of Convention: General or Limited?

A general convention is one where all and *any* amendments proposed by the States are accepted and considered for ratification. A limited convention is where the States predetermine the issues to be addressed and only amendments regarding those issues are considered for ratification. The question is what body actually governs the process? Who maintains the limited or general convention?

The Congressional assertions, as shown by this CRS Summary, place Congress in a position of supremacy over the States in an Article V convention. I believe that we can see, through this CRS report, that Congress has no intentions of allowing the States to have any control over the convention.

The CRS summary shows Congress believes that the kind of convention they call really depends upon one deciding factor: who has supremacy in the convention, Congress or the States. Consider the following:

The CRS notes that the language of Article V is broadly inclusive; "...*on application of the legislatures of two thirds of the Several States, Congress shall call a convention for proposing Amendments...*"[99] This places no limitation on the number and scope of Amendments that would be considered by the convention. One of the scholars chosen by the Congress to help formulate their argument asserts that limited conventions would be constitutionally impermissible, because no language found in Article V authorizes a limited convention. He states, *"Congress can't be obliged, no matter how many States ask for it, to summon a convention for limited purposes."*[100] This means, as the CRS points out, any number of State applications for a convention that make application for specific amendments are null and void.

On the other hand Walter Dellinger, former Solicitor General, advised Congress in 1979 that if the States want to trespass any original limitations on the convention then they have the power to do so;

"...any new Constitutional Convention must have the authority to study, debate, and submit to the States for ratification whatever amendments it considers appropriate...if the legislatures of thirty-four States request Congress to call a general convention, Congress has a Constitutional duty to summon such a convention, if those thirty-four States so recommend in their applications that the convention consider only a particular subject, Congress must call a convention and leave to the convention the ultimate determination of the agenda and the nature of the amendments it may choose to propose."[101]

According to past actions and conclusions of Congress, as presented by the CRS, Congress believes the only sure way to guarantee the convention structure is to place Congress in control of the amendment procedure. Congress will then be the governing body of the Convention, making sure all the States stay on track within the proposed limitations, either general or limited. Then what we have done is place Congress in a position superior to the States AGAIN! Then Congress will be in the position to determine from day one, regardless of the wishes of the States, that we will have a convention based on Congress' own limits because that is the avenue that gives them the most power and control

In fact the CRS asserts that allowing the convention to be supreme over Congress, and consequently supreme over the entire federal government, would create a general convention, not a limited one.

"In this theory, a convention is, a premier assembly of the people, a representative body charged by the people with the duty of framing the basic law of the land, for which purpose there devolves upon it all the power which the people themselves possess…The Convention is possessed of sovereign powers and is therefore supreme to all other government branches and agencies."[102] US Congress, House of Representatives, Committee on the Judiciary, Cyril Brickfield, 1957.

Ultimately the States' views are moot, since the CRS asserts that Congress believes it has the authority to control the scope and content of any convention, limited or otherwise.

"Congress, however, has historically sought to provide for limited conventions…Once valid applications are received from thirty-four States, Congress has maintained the call for an Article V must come from Congress, and Congress has the authority to limit the subject of Amendments to be considered."[103]

The CRS says this requires a "balance of authority." The States are authorized to apply for a limited convention, but only Congress can guarantee by law the scope and content of the convention.

The Senate Judiciary Committee in 1984 claimed for Congress the power both to set and enforce limits on the subject or subjects considered by a convention. The Goldwater Institute, according to the CRS summary, agrees with this claim of power for Congress stating that Congress holds the power and authority to enforce any kind of convention requested by the States.[104] Therefore, according to Congress and the CRS, the only real guaranteed protection against a "run-away convention" is complete Congressional control. Yet another example of "Trust us, we know better than you. We should be in control."

It is really interesting how the CRS ends their discussion on the kind of convention we would have. The CRS says, even after all the discussion, "what kind of convention" Congress will call won't be known until Congress actually calls a convention. In other words, we must call the convention to know what will be in the convention. That path should sound eerily familiar and should give us great pause before traveling it again.

The next question Congress is going to address and answer, now that we have a convention and it has met, is whether Congress is required to accept all amendments proposed by the States in an Article V convention. The CRS reminds us of the precedent established from the 1970's to the 1990's, through proposed legislation, indicating that Congress believes they can reserve the right to decide whether an amendment or amendments proposed by a convention should be circulated to the States for approval and ratification.[105] If you believe in a limited convention, then Congress says you must give them the authority to deny the convention the ability to submit any and all amendments.

A CRS report from 1984 states that the Senate has asserted the *"the convention is without authority to propose any amendment or amendments of a subject matter different than that set forth in the concurrent resolutions calling for the convention. In other words, the convention, although a sovereign body, is subject to the limitations of the concurrent resolution by Congress…"[106]* (emphasis mine)

In order to have a limited convention, Congress believes it has the power to set the procedures and set the criteria for a valid amendment. A limited convention requires a powerful governing Congress. But, as Senator Sam Erivin, Jr. asserted, *"unlimited power in the Congress to refuse to submit proposed Amendments for ratification would destroy the independence of the convention."[107]* Without a governing Congress, the Congress asserts, there is no way to guarantee a limited convention. But to get a limited convention, the States must surrender the independence of the convention.

According to the CRS, the Goldwater Institute believes that Congress must send on to the States all amendments proposed and it is up to the States to limit themselves. Do we still have a limited convention if the States decide not to limit themselves? The CRS then claims the Goldwater Institute proposes that any amendment offered in a convention, beyond the scope of the convention, could be viewed as "policy recommendations" to Congress.[108] So, Congress can decide which amendments are truly amendments and which are "policy recommendations." That should give them some interesting wiggle room!

Will Congress be merely a clerk for the convention or its controlling authority? After all, the power to make laws is vested solely in Congress. And according to the Congressional precedent and material, Article V gives Congress the power to call a convention and impose requirements on the convention as to its form, procedures, and agenda. The CRS also reminds us that Congress has historically interpreted its authority to "call" as a broad mandate to establish standards and procedures for the entire Article V process. So does Congress have to submit all amendments for ratification or not?

The CRS ends the report on whether Congress must submit all amendments proposed by the convention much in the same way they ended the discussion on the question, what kind of convention; by answering the question with a question.

"Ultimately the question of whether Congress can refuse to propose an amendment may also depend upon the answer to the previous question, what manner of convention does Article V authorize."[109]

If it is a limited convention, Congress has asserted Congressional power to judge and determine which amendments are valid. But what kind of convention will it be? Remember, we won't know until we call one!

What is the president's role in Article V?

Another question: What does Congress believe the role of the president to be in Article V?

It is a very interesting question, very interesting that Congress would even ask it. The CRS admits the most obvious answer to that question is that the president has no role at all. He is not mentioned in Article V and he is not delegated any authority or responsibilities. But you know it can't and won't end there. With politicians and political power on the line it is never that cut and dry.

The CRS is quick to point out that there are some compelling arguments that the president actually has an important role to play. Believe it or not, the entire argument, giving the president power in Article V, is based upon the amount of power Congress holds in the convention. According to this argument, the more power *Congress* holds in a convention, the more justification exists for the president to have "veto power." Need we be reminded that the whole purpose of the Article V convention was to *fix* the federal government which was created by the Sovereign States to begin with? Time and time again, the federal government is placing itself in the master position and subjecting the States to their own process!

The argument is that the convention will have the "force of law" and Article 1 section 7 clause 3 mandates:

"Every order, resolution, or vote to which the concurrence of the Senate and House of Representatives may be necessary (except on a question of adjournment) shall be presented to the President of the United States; and before the same shall take effect, shall be approved by him, or being disapproved by him, shall be repassed by two thirds of the Senate and House of Representatives, according to the rules and limitations prescribed in the case of a bill."[110]

Since Article V has the force of law, this argument states that Article 1 section 7 clause 3 cannot be avoided. This position also claims that since Congress's obligation to "call" a convention is clearly a power to spell out the specific terms of the convention, those terms would be similar to the general kinds of legislation that Congress normally deals with. So, this legislative act, according to the CRS, is no different than any other and would require presidential approval.[111] The CRS openly admits there is NOTHING in Article V regarding this.

They say *"there can be little doubt that the Congress is possessed with the authority to issue legislation on the subject matter of the "Constitutional Convention Implementation Act."[112]* Therefore, Article 1 section 7 clause 3 will naturally INCLUDE the President in the Article V process.

Isn't that great!? We not only will have a power struggle between Congress and the States, but we will also have the executive branch attempting to interject itself into the process.

Let me close with another interesting question to consider. What does Congress believe is the proper number and selection of delegates? CRS points out that the formula used to determine the number of delegates is commonly considered the same as for the Electoral College.[113] But are we guaranteed that is how it will work? Who will determine the number and procedure? I think we know if Congress gets its way, they will answer both those questions.

But a more important question may be, "could Senators or Representatives be delegates?" The CRS notes that Article 1 section 6 clause 2 of the Constitution prohibits Senators and Representatives from being appointed to any civil office while holding their office. The House judiciary committee recognized in 1993 that if members of Congress could be delegates, it would constitute a great potential for conflict of interest;[114] these members would be the regulators and the regulated!

However, in true political form, we have a loophole. CRS lets us know that Congress can reasonably claim there is no Constitutional prohibition against members of Congress serving as delegates. In 1974, the American Bar Association "ruled" that the mandate in Article 1 section 7 clause 3 prohibits Congress from holding office in one of the three branches of US government. But since a State delegate is outside this prohibition, there is no reason why a Congressman can't be a delegate as well.[115]

And now we have come full circle. James Madison warned us in Federalist #49, that if we were to hold a convention today the very same people in government that created the problem could be the very same people tasked to fix the problem. Madison warned us that this would not work out well for us. He said our convention would be taken over by political and personal motivations, rather than motivations for the preservation of Liberty.

The only question that remains is this...What kind of convention do you want? One that is completely controlled by Congress and subsequently the executive branch, or one where the sovereignty of the States remains and the States are in control?

Congress says, if you want a limited convention, the only way to guarantee that is to give them control. How do you think that will work out for us?

The argument in favor of an Article V convention of the States has rapidly advanced in the past few years. The Compact For America (CFA), a domestic non-profit "501(c)4" corporation, has a plan that is comprised of the Compact for a Balanced Budget Amendment ("the Compact"), a proposed interstate compact, which, in the words of its proponents, would transform *the otherwise cumbersome state-initiated amendment process under Article V into a 'turn-key' operation.*[116] The Compact is a comprehensive answer to all the Article V questions posed by offering a "contract" between the participating States to establish the rules and operations "missing" from the text of Article V, thus taking that function away from Congress and putting it into the hands of the States. This compact between the States would assert the States as the controlling parties in the convention and remove enormous power from the hands of Congress. This perspective is completely contrary to the understanding of Article V that Congress has presented over the years. And a recently published version of the CRS Summary on Article V shows that Congress has taken notice and will not relinquish their power without a fight.

CRS published an updated Summary on April 11, 2014, with the same title as the previous document.[117] This version addresses some issues that have developed since their last publication, to include the CFA compact. The CRS points out to Congress that this CFA compact is a "self-described interstate compact" and as such must fall under the authority of Article 1 section 10 clause 3 of the Constitution, otherwise known as the "Compact Clause." This is functionally a Congressional "check-mate" of the State sovereignty assertion. The Compact Clause reads in part:

*"No State shall, **without the Consent of the Congress**... enter into any Agreement or compact with another State...."[118]* (emphasis mine)

The CFA compact offers an agreement between the States to stop Congress from co-opting the convention process. Congress will respond to this denial of their power with the Compact Clause and say "you can't have this contract without our approval." And once again, Congress is not circumvented, but inserted into this process with overriding power over the States. What will be the recourse to resolving this power struggle? No doubt a law suit in federal court. What will be the result of a law suit in federal court where the judges are appointed by the same Congress that is a party to their case? Well, I'm sure it is quite obvious that it is not likely to be in favor of the sovereignty of the States.

Before we open our Constitution up for the tinkerers to perform open heart surgery, we might want to have a serious discussion about how we will safeguard against some of the clear and present dangers lurking in the operating room.

PART II

ULTIMATE SAFEGUARDS

7. Tyrannized Enough Already

Americans need to understand that the Revolutionary War was not simply about taxes. History has proven that people are slow to resist tyranny in the name of money. Financial concerns may *stir* outrage, but it can never sustain a resistance to the spread of tyranny. Primarily, because governments are able to expand dependency and disperse enough goodies to appease the citizens.

Heavy Taxes

America in 1776 was no exception. In the French and Indian War, Great Britain had incurred a large debt defending the colonies. The government needed to recoup that debt. They decided to impose consumption taxes upon the colonists. The items taxed were things the colonists needed and used on a daily basis; linen, lumber, tea, sugar, paper, ink, etc. Unfortunately, the American colonists were expected to bear this tax burden while the rest of the empire enjoyed the fruits of colonial labor.

No Voice

Back in parliament the taxes were levied without the colonists having any voice in the matter. They rejected the notion that people in Parliament had "volunteered" to represent the colonists' interests. **They understood that if the men claiming to represent them never had to live under nor submit to the laws they created, they were NOT truly representatives of the people!** They KNEW that when the lawmakers who make the laws, can exempt themselves from the laws, those lawmakers do not and CANNOT truly represent them.

Mandates

Parliament paid no mind to the colonists concerns and didn't stop with just consumption taxes. To maximize their revenue from the colonists, they decided to not only tax these items, but also to *mandate* the colonists purchase those taxed items from approved sources. The colonists opposed these taxes and the laws being created to enforce them. They saw this as a form of slavery and systematic impoverishment.

Economic Enslavement

As one colonist put it, *"But if our Trade is to be curtailed in its most profitable Branches, & Burdens beyond all possible Bearing, laid upon that which is suffered to remain, we shall be so far from being able to take off the manufactures of Great Britain, that it will be scarce possible for us to earn our Bread...?"[119]* Samuel Adams

Samuel Adams went onto explain that the act of arbitrary taxation makes slaves out of a free people:

*"For if our Trade may be taxed why not our Lands? Why not the Produce of our Lands & every thing [sic] we possess or make use of? This we apprehend annihilates our **Charter Right to govern & tax ourselves**--It strikes at our British Privileges, which as we have never forfeited them, we hold in common with our Fellow Subjects who are Natives of Britain: If Taxes are laid upon us in any shape*

without our having a legal Representation where they are laid, are we not reduced from the Character of free Subjects to the miserable State of tributary Slaves?"[20] [emphasis added]

Samuel Adams saw the big picture. He knew that if the king assumed the power to lay taxes contrary to the common rights of the colonists, without giving the people any voice, there would be no limit to the power of this government.

Invasion of Privacy and Property

To enforce these laws, Parliament granted the government agents the power to search and seize from the colonists' homes and businesses with warrantless searches called "Writs of Assistance."

An Awakening

James Otis, Jr., a government attorney, was charged with the power and duty to enforce these laws and prosecute those who were brought into custody through these warrantless searches. The interesting thing is that James Otis, Jr, woke up! James Otis, Jr. was raised a patriot and began to feel conflicted by his government job. He understood the British Liberty Charters, Common Law, and the value of Liberty. He quickly realized that these oppressive and lawless acts were violations of the traditions of Liberty the British subjects had enjoyed for centuries, having secured them through years of conflict with the crown. As a result, Otis resigned his position and began to inform the people of the tyrannical actions of their own government.

Otis decided to confront the government in their tyranny by taking up a legal battle to end the power of the Writs of Assistance. Once Otis took up this legal battle, the powers that be conveniently "forgot" that Otis "resigned" and charged him with "abandonment" of his post; a charge that meant treason and was punishable by death. Otis was also cast out by his community; called everything but a good man. He was told he would never practice law in the Kingdom again. In his response to all these slanders, Otis gives us a sublime definition of "sacred honor:"

"I have been charged with desertion from my office. To this charge I can give a very sufficient answer. I renounced that office...I have taken more pains in this cause than I ever will take again, although my engaging in this...has raised much resentment. But I think I can sincerely declare that I cheerfully submit myself to every odious name for conscience' sake; and from my soul I despise those whose guilty, malice, or folly has made them my foes. Let the consequences be what they will, I am determined to proceed. The only principles of public conduct that are worthy of a gentleman or a man are to sacrifice estate, ease, health, and applause, and even life, to the sacred calls of his country."[21]

James Otis, Jr. stepped out, practically a lone man in defense of Liberty. He argued for 5 hours against these Writs of Assistance. He called them the *"worst instruments of arbitrary power"* the *"most destructive of English Liberty ever found in an English law book."[22]* He suffered the condemnation of his society and his profession all alone...or so he thought.

The Brushfire Is Lit

Forty years later, John Adams would write about that day in court with James Otis, Jr.

"But Otis was a flame of fire! With a promptitude of classical allusions, a depth of research, a rapid summary of historical events and dates, a profusion of legal authorities, a prophetic glare of his eyes into (the future), and a rapid torrent of impetuous eloquence, he hurried away all before him. American Independence was then and there born. The seeds of Patriots and Heroes – to defend the vigorous youth, were then and there sown. Every man of an immense, crowded audience, appeared to me to go away, as I did, ready to take up arms against Writs of Assistance. Then, and there, was the first scene of the first act of opposition to the arbitrary claims of Great Britain – then and there, the child of independence was born. In fifteen years, namely in 1776, he grew up to manhood and declared himself free."[23]

Adams, there and then asserted, *"I will to my dying day oppose, with all the powers and faculties God has given me, all the instruments of slavery on the one hand and villainy on the other as this Writs of Assistance is."[24]*

James Otis, Jr. stood for Liberty because he believed it to be his duty, not because he was cheered on by a big crowd. This one man standing alone sparked a spirit that would change the entire world.

With the clarity that history provides we can see that James Otis, Jr. was not alone in that courtroom that day. He was being watched by Samuel Adams, John Adams, Richard Henry Lee, Patrick Henry, and many of the men who would BECOME Liberty for the new nation.

Independent Media

From that courtroom Samuel Adams left so super charged that he formed the Committees of Correspondence; groups that would be established throughout the colonies to educate beyond the government controlled media, unite Liberty minded patriots, and fight for Liberty. Adams proposed the creation of these groups to disseminate TRUTH to prevent the government from *"perverting the judgment of men."*[125]

The King controlled the media at that time, and Liberty-minded colonists had grown tired of the propaganda. They wanted to educate each other on the truth in the face of government-controlled lies. Their first publication was a booklet called *"The Boston Pamphlet,"*[126] A series of reports outlining colonists' rights & Parliament's infringements upon those rights.

Protests

Because of the education provided to the colonists through these Committees of Correspondence, Samuel Adams also formed the first Political Action Committee...called the "Sons of Liberty." They began protesting these laws and the unlawful unconstitutional acts of their government, but their protests were a little different than ours. They held mock hangings of their government officials, mock funeral processions of their tax collectors and customs agents. They made these people feel ASHAMED for what they were doing. Perhaps that is why our "protests" have had little effect; we are not making our politicians feel ashamed for their behavior. Perhaps we are still too steeped in our cult of personality worship and love of party.

The most famous action of the Sons of Liberty was the Boston Tea Party. The Boston Tea Party sparked a chain of events that would alter the face of the world forever.

Legal Clamp-Down

In response to the colonists' actions, the British government had to act quickly and decisively to put an end to the uprisings in Boston. And as tyrants normally do, their reaction was as predictable as they were more tyrannical. Parliament passed a series of acts, one which closed the port of Boston, enacted on 1 June 1774[127]. A series of punitive acts, which we know as the Intolerable Acts, would be next. These three acts, together with the Quebec Act and the Quartering Act, are all together known as the "Coercive Acts," all crafted to increase government control over the people through regulation.

The driving force for the Coercive Acts, was another piece of legislation called the "Declaratory Act," passed March 18, 1766. It stated that Parliament *"had, hath, and of right ought to have, full power and authority to make laws and statutes of sufficient force and validity to bind the colonies and people of America, subjects of the crown of Great Britain, in all cases whatsoever."*[128] In effect, the British government had declared itself to be all powerful, and outside any criticism, punishable by a charge of treason and death. By doing this, they completely abandoned the façade of "representation" in Parliament. To put this in perspective, the government had just declared for itself the power to make and enforce any law, and then wrote laws that gave the government the authority to enforce those laws with armed force. This, as you might imagine, did not sit well with the colonists – and the king knew this!

Give Up Your Guns!

In May of 1774, the king appointed General Thomas Gage military Royal Governor over Massachusetts.[129] Gage would become very aggressive in the efforts to control the colonists and subdue their "seditious" behavior. Under the King's orders, Gage was going to enforce the "Coercive Acts" upon the colonists whether they liked it or not.[130]

Gage passed laws that forbade any town meetings without his approval and would only legally allow one town meeting a year. The colonists did not submit to such violations of their rights quietly. They did not "go along to get along." They assembled anyway and let the "consequences be as they may." The consequences were that Gage sent troops to disband one of these assemblies in Salem, Ma. The people, outraged at this overt display of force, responded by gathering over 3,000 armed colonists, causing Gage's men to retreat. This would not be the end of Gage's tyrannical aggression.

Gage was told by the King to get the colonists under control. But Gage did not have the force necessary to control the colonists, because the colonists outnumbered Gage's troops and out-armed them as well. But Gage found a solution to this problem: **take control of the gun powder and ammunition.**

Early morning on September 1, 1774, Gage's troops seized hundreds of barrels of gun powder from the Charleston powder house.[131]   The colonists did not respond by standing in line to turn over their arms and ammunition. They saw Gage's actions as a show of force; an act of war against the colonists and their God given rights. The colonists responded by banding together. By the end of the day, men whose ages spanned 16-60 and numbered upwards of *twenty thousand*, were marching to Boston to support their Liberty. The colonists were now going to "ready themselves" in **defense** of their Liberty.

Just five days after Gage's act of war against the colonists, the militia of Worchester County replaced all leaders appointed by the king with those chosen by the people.

The same day the people of Suffolk County issued a list of nineteen grievances against the government. They took control of the militia away from the Gage and announced they were going to have open arms training every day.

The representatives of the people were not silent. They were also outraged by Gage's behavior and unanimously endorsed the Suffolk grievances. These politicians then encouraged all other colonies to send aid to those in Boston. All this was done before the internet and cell phones! Only five days have passed since Governor Gage took the gun powder from one city in Massachusetts.

The Earl of Dartmouth, the Royal Secretary of State for America again ordered Gage to disarm the people.[132] Gage told Dartmouth that it would not be possible to control the colonists without force.[133] Dartmouth then sent a letter to George III asking to have all import of weapons and ammunition to the colonies stopped. **George fulfilled this request by requiring a permit for all exports of arms and ammunition from Great Britain and then simply refused to issue those permits.**[134]

In response to the colonists stand against the government, Governor Gage ordered his men to conduct warrantless searches on the colonists, ordering them to seize all their arms and ammunition.

The Boston chapter of the Committees of Correspondence received information that the government was getting ready to seize all the ammunition, arms, and cannons from fort William and Mary. In response, the militia rapidly organized and were able to secure their property before the government troops could take it from them.

At this point, Parliament became really concerned. The reports they were receiving relayed that there were three million colonists: all angry, all armed and all ready to defend themselves. They were not certain that they had sufficient government force to subdue such numbers.

At about the same time, on March 23, 1775, Patrick Henry gave his famous "Give me Liberty or Give me Death" speech in St. Johns Church. Following that speech a committee was formed to issue the Resolutions of the Provincial Congress of Virginia. This Resolution called for the organization of the people into armed groups to keep the government form seizing their property and enforcing the laws that violated their Liberty. The Resolution read:

"Resolved, that a well-regulated militia composed of gentlemen and yeomen is the natural strength and only security of a free government, that such a militia in this colony would forever render it unnecessary for the mother country to keep among us, for the purpose of our defence, any standing army of mercenary forces, always subversive of the quiet, and dangerous to the liberties of the people, and would obviate the pretext of taxing us for their support....

...Resolved therefore, that this colony be immediately put into a posture of defence: and that Patrick Henry, Richard Henry Lee, Robert Carter Nicholas, Benjamin Harrison, Lemuel Riddick, George Washington, Adam Stephen, Andrew Lewis, William Christian, Edmund Pendleton, Thomas Jefferson and Isaac Zane, Esquires, be a committee to prepare a plan for the embodying arming and disciplining such a number of men as may be sufficient for that purpose."[35]

What these resolutions effectively did was attempt to remove the reason for keeping soldiers in the Virginia Colony at all. "You want security and peace? No problem, we'll take care of it, send your soldiers home."

General Gage had another plan, however. In the early morning of April 19, 1775, he sent out regiments of British soldiers to Lexington to capture Samuel Adams and John Hancock, then on to Concord to seize gunpowder. But spies and friends of the colonists leaked word of Gage's plan, Paul Revere went on a ride, and the colonists were waiting. What resulted came to be known as the "shot heard 'round the world."

February 14, 1776 Thomas Paine would publish "Common Sense". In this pivotal pamphlet, Paine references that day in April:

"No man was a warmer wisher for reconciliation than myself, before the fatal nineteenth of April 1775, but the moment the event of that day was made known, I rejected the hardened, sullen tempered Pharaoh of England for ever; and disdain the wretch, that with the pretended title of FATHER OF HIS PEOPLE, can unfeelingly hear of their slaughter, and composedly sleep with their blood upon his soul."[36]

For Patrick Henry and many others, reconciliation with the king was no longer an option. They now understood that the King had no intention of treating the colonists as anything but cows to be milked. Independence was now their only solution. The people KNEW that the right to keep and bear arms was essential to the preservation of Liberty. They KNEW that if the government could disarm them, they would be like every other nation in Europe, subjects and slaves. They KNEW that independence from this tyranny was the ONLY way to ensure *real* Liberty.

And what sparked this whole course of events?

ONE Governor took the arms and ammunition from ONE city in Massachusetts!

8. To Keep And Bear Arms

The history in the preceding chapter lays the foundation for the proper understanding of the need for the Right to Keep and Bear Arms. The absence of this historical perspective has left a large swath of Americans ignorant to the importance of this *ultimate safeguard of life, liberty and property.* In fact, that history demonstrates not just the right, but the **sovereign duty** of the people to keep and bear arms, for the security of a free State.

I sincerely believe that there are those who DO know this history and that is EXACTLY WHY they want to take our guns. Fortunately, the issue of "gun rights" crosses party lines and many Americans are passionate about this issue and have not submitted to overt attacks. By slow degrees, however, the opposition has attempted to whittle away our God-given right to protect ourselves from tyranny. The more ignorance abounds, the easier their task is of removing such a necessary safeguard from the hands of the citizenry.

This ignorance surrounding the Second Amendment illustrates the broader problem in America of misinterpreting the Constitution. If you don't know where these protections came from, you won't understand the relevance of them today. This is part of the reason for many of the naïve arguments given today against the Second Amendment. Indeed, all the way back in the Grand Remonstrance of 1641[137] Liberty loving people declared that a mechanism of "malignant and pernicious design" is the disarming of the people while the government remained armed. This is not a new trapping of tyranny. Centuries of a "long train of abuses" brought our framers to the conclusion that securing the right of the people to possess arms was necessary within the Bill of Rights.

Common Sense Debate

Some say we need to redefine the terms within the Second Amendment because we live in a different world. They say our framers could not have possibly known the type of weapons that would be developed by modern society. Therefore the framers could not have possibly meant that the "right of the people to keep and bear arms" would be without limit. Notwithstanding, that the muskets the framers had were the most advanced weapons of their time, we must remember that the framers were applying *principles*, not drafting laws for specific circumstances. Knowing the history and circumstances that brought our founders to incorporate the Second Amendment into the Bill of Rights, is the only way we can have a "common sense debate" on gun related issues in modern times. In truth we get plenty of debate and little common sense.

It seems that nearly every anti-gun conversation consists of a litany of alleged reasons why we don't need particular firearms or any firearms in general. You don't need a gun to protect yourself, it is asserted, you have the police. Of course, the police don't live at my house and it'll be quite a drive for them to make it to me if an armed intruder decides to pay a visit. I suppose instead of my .45 caliber pistol, I could instead keep a stockpile of milk and cookies and encourage the assailant to kick back and enjoy them until the police arrive.

We are told that "Most people end up being killed with their own handgun," as if it is some consolation to be killed with the gun that the intruder brought with him instead. I am sure the last thing that goes through the mind of the home invasion victim is "Boy, I am sure glad he just shot me with his own gun instead of the handgun I was smart enough not to own!"

We are told that we could not possibly arm our schools, we don't want guns around our children! Instead we are left to pray that the closets and desks will protect them until the perp runs out of ammo or shoots himself.

Some are generous, however, and will allow the notion that we may want to shoot skeet or an occasional squirrel for sport. While sport is fine to engage in, we are assured by those who would rule us that the right to bear arms is far from essential in our modern society. Yet, we can be trust this one thing, it was not squirrels who kicked the doors in late at night and dragged dissenters to the gulag in the Soviet Union. Even the most ardent conspiracy theorist doesn't believe it's the squirrels that are tapping your phones, seizing your property, bankrupting your children, reading your emails, arming your local police with military hardware, making kill lists, selling weapons to Al Qaeda while labeling vets, Christians and Jews as the greatest threat to American safety. No silly rabbit, guns are not for squirrels. They are essential to the preservation of Liberty!

However, the right to bear arms is not only an essential Liberty, but an inherent one. Sam Adams wrote in 1772;

"Among the natural rights of the Colonists are these: First, a right to life; Secondly, to liberty; Thirdly, to property; together with the right to support and defend them in the best manner they can."[138]

Without the "right to support and defend" our rights, they cannot be secure!

It is sometimes stunning to realize that some of the very people we have entrusted to secure these rights are so frighteningly misguided as to the real meaning of the Second Amendment and their duty to support and defend it. For example, Sheriff Jim Coates, the leader of the Florida Association of Sheriffs, testifying before the State Senate made this comment: *"The Florida Sheriff's Association supports the Second Amendment, the Constitutional right of the people to bear arms...I understand it's about people's rights, but people's rights need to be **granted** in a responsible way, for the right reasons."[139]* (emphasis mine)

This Constitutionally established law enforcement officer believes that rights are "granted" and furthermore should be "granted" only for the "right reasons." In 1776, when we became Independent from Great Britain, the government stopped having the authority to "grant" rights. When we became a Constitutional Republic, We The People declared that all the rights belong to the people and that the government receives its just powers from the consent of the governed. Oh, how the tables have turned!

We must understand that there is no such thing as a "common sense debate on gun legislation." The gun-grabbers do not want to legislate away guns, they just want to legislate them out of the hands of ordinary citizens. According to the Washington Times, even Diane Feinstein possesses these "forbidden" firearms, to include a Bushmaster XM-15, Tec-9 handgun, Smith & Wesson M&P15 and a Glock 19 with a "high-capacity" magazine![140]

When we cut out all the manipulation and politics, what is really being discussed is not GUN control, but PEOPLE control. We must understand that we are not talking about "gun legislation," we are talking "Second Amendment legislation." The Second Amendment cannot be constitutionally altered through the simple legislative process as they are suggesting. And yet, it has been done illegally throughout our nation's history.

Truth be told, the manipulators don't want you to know the *simplicity* of the Second Amendment. The words "shall not be infringed" are pretty clear and self-explanatory. But those hungry for power and bent on constraining and controlling Liberty cannot admit that. I recently asked Minnesota gubernatorial candidate, Scott Honor, what he thought the words "shall not be infringed" meant. I was not surprised that he was reluctant to even answer that question. Because the definitions are so simple that lawmakers, even future ones, are hesitant to give up their "wiggle room."

The word "shall" is a binding directive used to express what is mandatory. Shall not, simply means it is mandatory that it NOT happen; absolutely forbidden. The word "infringed" means to violate. So to take this all in context, "shall not be infringed" simply means it is absolutely forbidden to violate. It's not rocket science. Once politicians admit that the words mean absolutely forbidden to not violate, then they know they then cannot have a "gun legislation debate," with or without "common sense."

It's not just the meaning of the words "shall not be infringed" that is essential to the proper application of the Second Amendment, but we must also know WHY our framers felt it necessary to identify the right to keep and bear arms as an essential Liberty. And once again, the reason is easily established by the men who wrote the Amendment.

George Mason, the Father of our Bill of Rights, explained on June 14, 1788;

*"Forty years ago, when the resolution of **enslaving America** was formed in Great Britain, the British Parliament was advised by an artful man, who was governor of Pennsylvania, **to disarm the people**; that it was the **best and most effectual way to enslave** them; but that they should not do it openly, but weaken them, and let them sink gradually..."*[41]

Mr. Mason wanted us to know that the only way a people can become enslaved is if they are disarmed. Mason knew it just as well as the King of Great Britain!

Noah Webster, the author of Webster's Dictionary and an essential founder of American Liberty, wrote in 1788;

*"**Before a standing army can rule, the people must be disarmed;** as they are in almost every kingdom of Europe. The supreme power in America cannot enforce unjust laws by the sword; because the whole body of the people are armed, and constitute a force superior to any bands of regular troops that can be, on any pretense, raised in the United States. A military force, at the command of Congress, can execute no laws, but such as the people perceive to be just and constitutional; for they will possess the power, and jealousy will instantly inspire the inclination, to resist the execution of a law which appears to them unjust and oppressive."[142]* (emphasis mine)

Mr. Webster wanted us to know that the only way we will keep the government from enforcing unjust, oppressive, and unconstitutional laws would be that the WHOLE BODY of the people be armed with a force SUPERIOR to the government.

Richard Henry Lee, who is believed to be the author of the Letters of a Federal Farmer, warned in Letter #18;

*"...whereas, **to preserve liberty,** it is **essential** that the **whole body** of the people **always possess arms,** and be taught alike, especially when young, how to use them; nor does it follow from this, that all promiscuously must go into actual service on every occasion. The mind that aims at a select militia, must be influenced by a truly*

anti-republican principle; and when we see many men disposed to practice upon it, whenever they can prevail, no wonder true republicans are for carefully guarding against it."[143] (emphasis mine)

We also have Patrick Henry cautioning us in 1788:

"*O sir, we should have fine times, indeed, if, to punish tyrants, it were only sufficient to assemble the people!* **Your arms**, *wherewith you could defend yourselves,* **are gone**...*Did you ever read of* **any revolution in a nation**, *brought about by the punishment of those in power,* **inflicted by those who had no power at all?**"[144]

Our framers were not afraid that we would be disarmed by deer and rabbits. They did not believe that sportsmen and collectors would disarm us. They didn't even fear that the criminals would organize to take our guns so they could keep them all to themselves. Our framers feared our own GOVERNMENT would become the criminals that would disarm and enslave us. They attempted to sound the alarm and put government on notice that we bear arms to preserve Liberty and keep from becoming enslaved by an unjust, oppressive, and unconstitutional government with an unlawful standing army.

You do not have to be a Harvard Law grad or be Oxford-trained to get this. As a matter of fact, it is probably better if you are not. So why do we have so many in government, even those who claim to be "Constitutional conservatives," fundamentally ignorant as to the proper meaning and application of this essential Liberty? Why is it that even on the local level we have to defend this Liberty from attack by the very authorities who we entrust to protect it? Is it possible that those we have vested with that trust are unworthy of it?

Samuel Adams warned us, *"if we suffer tamely a lawless attack upon our liberty, we encourage it, and involve others in our doom." It is a very serious consideration ... that millions yet unborn may be the miserable sharers of the event."*[145] We have tamely suffered frequent attacks on this fundamental Liberty. We have accepted government imposed permits, background checks, and limitations on our right to keep and bear arms. How does it make any sense that we have to *ask permission* from the government as to when and where we can carry guns, when they are the *reason* we bear arms? Isn't it time we learn from our history? Isn't it time we listen to *real* wisdom and support and defend our own Liberty?

9 The Right To Resist

A prominent media personality has said that God never calls someone to act in anger. If that's so we must ignore the fact that in John 2:15 Jesus himself got angry at the money changers in the temple and made a whip and began overturning tables driving people out of the temple :

"And when he had made a scourge of small cords, he drove them all out of the temple, and the sheep, and the oxen; and poured out the changers' money, and overthrew the tables;" -John 2:15 (KJV)

Although the Bible teaches that anger **without cause** is akin to murder, anger itself is not a sin. If this were not so, then Jesus sinned in the temple that day and God the Father also sinned, as the Bible is replete with testimony of God's anger and the expression of His wrath as well as Him directing His people to act with lethal force to carry out justice (certainly in the Old Testament). But that anger was never without cause. There was a REASON for that anger.

There is a **right** to resist oppression inherent in our nature as free people. It should make us angry when abuses, usurpations, and oppressions remove the Liberty that has been given to us by God. The framers of this nation knew this, and so did David when he fought Goliath, Elijah when he challenged King Ahab for stealing Naboth's vineyard, Nathan when he challenged King David for his sin with Bathsheba, Samuel when he challenged King Saul for his disobedience to God. So did the Hebrew nursemaids when they refused to carry out government mandated abortions, Daniel when he refused to eat the Kings meat or to stop praying, the Hebrew boys when they resisted the executive order to bow to idols, the Apostles when they refused the local authorities' order to stop preaching the Gospel.

Resistance to tyranny is the DUTY of a Liberty loving, God-honoring people. I simply have to sigh at the premise offered by some in positions of authority and influence when they attempt to appear knowledgeable about certain events in history or certain perspectives of the framers and yet profess that revolution, secession or resistance is a form of lawlessness and rebellion. The notion that those who are taking a stand are godless rebels, seems to me to ignore the numerous examples of resistance to civil authority we find in the Scriptures. God did not make it a sin to resist tyranny. God made it clear he wants us to submit to LAWFUL AUTHORITY, not to tyranny. I don't believe the resistance we see today is an attempt to violently overthrow lawful authority. I see people taking a stand and not backing up, even if it means being tazed, body-slammed or beaten. The people have had enough of heavy handed federal overreach. It may mean we go into the fire like the three Hebrew boys in Daniel, but we've made up our minds, we WILL NOT BOW. For a full treatment of the issue of civil disobedience from a biblical perspective, I recommend the book *God Rather Than Men* by Pastor JC Hall.

Patrick Henry, in his wisdom asked these questions,

"Shall we resort to entreaty and humble supplication? What terms shall we find which have not been already exhausted? Let us not, I beseech you, sir, deceive ourselves. Sir, we have done everything that could be done, to avert the storm which is now coming on. We have petitioned; we have remonstrated; we have supplicated; we have prostrated ourselves before the throne, and have implored its interposition to arrest the tyrannical hands of the ministry and Parliament. Our petitions have been slighted; our remonstrances have produced additional violence and insult; our supplications have been disregarded; and we have been spurned, with contempt, from the foot of the throne...Shall we gather strength by irresolution and inaction? Shall we acquire the means of effectual resistance, by lying supinely on our backs, and hugging the delusive phantom of hope, until our enemies shall have bound us hand and foot?"[146]

Samuel Adams reminded us in 1772 that *"Among the natural rights of the Colonists are these: First, a right to life; Secondly, to liberty; Thirdly, to property; together with the right to support and defend them in the best manner they can."[147]* We believe, as our founders did, that we have a NATURAL RIGHT to defend life, Liberty and property from oppressive and tyrannical governments.

I don't believe these men and women were godless provocateurs. On the contrary, I believe they were God-fearing patriots committed to standing for what was right regardless of the consequences, even if it meant their friends and fellow countrymen mocked and disowned them. They knew they had a duty to God to resist unlawful authority as a testimony of the Righteousness of God. One wonders if this could be a reason for removing and ridiculing religious thought? Wouldn't government be best served by removing the understanding that there is a power higher than government?

Here are a series of statements from the founders of our nation and other wise men and women. Consider the following direct statements, old British spelling and all:

"That to secure these rights, Governments are instituted among Men, deriving their just powers from the consent of the governed, --That whenever any Form of Government becomes destructive of these ends, it is the **Right of the People to alter or to abolish it...***"[148] Declaration of Independence* (emphasis mine)

"To vindicate these rights when actually violated or attack'd, the subjects of England are entitled first to the regular administration and free course of justice in the courts of law—next to the right of petitioning the King and parliament for redress of grievances-and lastly, to the **right of having and using arms for self-preservation and defence.***"[149] Justice Blackstone* (emphasis mine)

"Everyone knows that the exercise of the military power is forever dangerous to civil rights; and we have had recent instances of violences that have been offer'd to private subjects, and the last week, even to a magistrate in the execution of his office!- Such violences are no more than might have been expected from military troops: A power, which is apt enough at all times to take a wanton lead, even when in the midst of civil society; but more especially so,

when they are led to believe that they are become necessary, to awe a spirit of rebellion, and preserve peace and good order. But there are some persons, who would, if possibly they could, perswade the people never to make use of their **constitutional rights** *or terrify them from doing it.*"[150] Samuel Adams (bold emphasis mine)

"*If the representatives of the people betray their constituents, there is then no resource left but in the exertion of that original* **right of self-defence, which is paramount to all positive forms of government...**"[151] *Alexander Hamilton* (emphasis mine)

"*But ambitious encroachments of the Foederal Government, on the authority of the State governments, would not excite the opposition of a single State or of a few States only. They would be signals of general alarm. Every Government would espouse the common cause. A correspondence would be opened.* **Plans of resistance** *would be concerted. One spirit would animate and conduct the whole...But what degree of madness could ever drive the Foederal Government to such an extremity?*"[152] *James Madison* (emphasis mine)

"*The* **spirit of resistance to government is so valuable** *on certain occasions, that* **I wish it to be always kept alive.** *It will often be exercised when wrong, but better so than not to be exercised at all. I like a little rebellion now and then. It is like a storm in the Atmosphere.*"[153] *Thomas Jefferson to Abigail Adams*

"*Let us contemplate our forefathers, and posterity, and resolve to maintain the rights bequeathed to us from the former, for the sake of the latter. The necessity of the times, more than ever, calls for our utmost circumspection, deliberation, fortitude and perseverance. Let us remember that "if we suffer tamely a lawless attack upon our liberty, we encourage it, and involve others in our doom." It is a very serious consideration … that millions yet unborn may be the miserable sharers of the event."*[154] Samuel Adams

"Before a standing army can rule, the people must be disarmed; as they are in almost every kingdom of Europe. The supreme power in America cannot enforce unjust laws by the sword; because the whole body of the people are armed, and constitute a force superior to any bands of regular troops that can be, on any pretense, raised in the United States. A military force, at the command of Congress, can execute no laws, but such as the people perceive to be just and constitutional; for they will possess the power, and jealousy will instantly inspire the inclination, to resist the execution of a law which appears to them unjust and oppressive."[155] Noah Webster

"The honorable gentleman who presides told us that, to prevent abuses in our government, we will assemble in Convention, recall our delegated powers, and punish our servants for abusing the trust reposed in them. O sir, we should have fine times, indeed, if, to punish tyrants, it were only sufficient to assemble the people! **Your arms, wherewith you could defend yourselves, are gone…** *Did you ever read of any revolution in a nation, brought about by the punishment of those in power, inflicted by those who had no power at all?"*[156] Patrick Henry

"May nothing ever check that glorious spirit of freedom which inspires the patriot in the cabinet, and the hero in the field, with courage to maintain their righteous cause, and to endeavor to transmit the claim to posterity, **even if they must seal the rich conveyance to their children with their own blood.***" "The principles of the*

revolution ought ever to be the pole-star of the statesmen, respected by the rising generation."[157] Mercy Otis Warren

*"Gentlemen may cry, Peace, Peace but there is no peace. The war is actually begun! The next gale that sweeps from the north will bring to our ears the clash of resounding arms! Our brethren are already in the field! Why stand we here idle? What is it that gentlemen wish? What would they have? Is life so dear, or peace so sweet, as to be purchased at the price of chains and slavery? Forbid it, Almighty God! I know not what course others may take; but as for me, **give me liberty or give me death!**"*[158]

Where do we go from here? Richard Henry Lee said the ratification debates have *"called forth the able advocates of liberty, and tends to renew, in the minds of the people, their true republican jealousy and vigilance, the strongest guard against the abuses of power;"*[159]

WE THE PEOPLE are charged with defending our Liberty, we are the strongest guard against the abuse of power. But even Mr. Lee knew, *"the vigilance of the people is not sufficiently constant to be depended on…"*[160]

Representative Mike Rogers, a Republican from Michigan recently said during the House Intelligence Committee hearing concerning NSA surveillance, *"you can't have your privacy violated if you don't know your privacy is violated, right?"*[161]

Perhaps Mr. Rogers is more correct than we would like to admit. Because if we do not know what our rights **are**; if we do not understand where they come from and why they are so important, we will have our Liberty stolen and we won't even know it.

That is why this education is so important. We The People must get educated and start defending...not only for ourselves, but for future generations who would enjoy the fruits of our own vigilance. Alexander Hamilton warned us:

"Is it not better, I ask, to suffer a few present inconveniences, than to put yourselves in the way of losing everything that is precious? Your lives, your property, your religion, are all at stake. I do my duty. I warn you of your danger. If you should still be so mad as to bring destruction upon yourselves; if you still neglect what you owe to God and man, you cannot plead ignorance in your excuse. Your consciences will reproach you for your folly; and your children's children will curse you."[162]

We The People Must have the courage and strength to stand against those who attempt to infringe upon the Liberties that are not be violated. But to stand we must know the purpose for these Amendments and the origins of our Liberty. We must GET EDUCATED about Liberty and the provenance of our freedom. We The People must be the defenders of Liberty and stop looking to government to protect a thing that doesn't belong to them, a thing they can never possess but can only usurp!

You have just been EDUCATED! Now spread the truth far and wide. Tell your neighbors, your family members, your legislators and your sheriffs...MY rights are a gift from God, not the endowment of governments. My Liberties SHALL NOT BE INFRINGED because I WILL TAKE UP MY **SOVEREIGN DUTY** TO DEFEND IT!

PART III

HOPE FOR THE FUTURE

10. Purpose

I have been traveling the country for 4 years now, teaching people the history of the founding of our nation. I do this because I believe two things: one, that I have a duty to God to steward the gift of Liberty and two, those who do not know their history are doomed to repeat its mistakes.

In my teaching I have been honored to teach on high school and college campuses. One event early in my teaching experience, in particular, stands out for me. I was able to spend two days with a room full of high school-aged, homeschooled students. It was amazing. The first day, we went through a practical exercise to teach both the difference between a democracy and a republic and the value of Liberty over security. The second day I taught them the Roots of Liberty Seminar that I normally give to adults.

I was particularly nervous about the second day. How would I relate this history and these complex principles to people who have had few real life experiences with the economy, adult society, and political concerns or responsibility? As it turned out, I would be the one who would get a lesson that day.

I had been teaching for over two years the understanding that Liberty is an inherent possession of man. But I more fully realized that fact as I spent two days with these young people. Because Liberty is inherent, teaching young people the value of Liberty was not as difficult as I had anticipated.

I saw the evidence of that awakening in their spirits as I shed light in their minds on this great gift from God. The first day they were able to experience that Liberty means something and that they would no longer be so flippant with its care. They really learned and understood what most of the people in government will never know and understand; Liberty can never be traded for security, not ever. Many went home after the first night and were enthusiastically telling their fathers all about the day's lessons. They were excited about what they had learned. They were excited that learning about history and government was so much fun. They were excited to know that they were going back to hear more the next day. I was as amazed as the parents were.

But the second day, through the lamp of history and the oracle of truth, they were able to understand why Liberty is worth so much. These young people were captivated by their history. For 5 hours, a room full of 30 or more high school students listened intently to the history and the foundation of their nation. They learned about the battles against tyranny by those who were beginning, like them, to understand that Liberty is their possession. They also learned they had a responsibility to defend Liberty from tyrants who would bully them into giving it away. They really got it. They really understood what 99% of our politicians don't. They now know that our nation was built with a purpose; the purpose to secure the blessings of Liberty for our posterity.

By the end of the day, my soul was so uplifted by their enthusiasm and patriotism; I could have stormed the doors of tyranny all by myself with a dull butter knife. But then it hit me. I paused long enough to look into their eager eyes, and it threw me to my knees. I was suddenly overwhelmed with sadness for what we have done to them, what we have given away on their behalf. I stopped my teaching and told them that I had to apologize. I suddenly realized the mess that we left behind for them. I was weeping in front of a room full of teenagers now, and I could not stop myself.

I looked into their eyes and realized, through our ignorance and our negligence, we have condemned them to purchase back a gift that was given to us; a gift that we were supposed to secure for them, not require them to secure for themselves. I got angry for a minute, but that anger made me even more resolved. I told them,

"Don't you dare use our negligence as an excuse. You go out and fight for what is rightfully yours. If the government tells you that you cannot speak, does that make you mute? If the government tells you that you cannot assemble, does that imprison you? If the government tells you that you cannot freely worship God, does that silence your soul?" To each question, with wide eyes, they responded "no." I told them, "Then do not be silenced, do not be imprisoned, and let your soul cry out. Because I promise you, from this day forward, I will do everything I am both humanly and supernaturally able to do to take back ground for you. I will do everything I can to make sure that you have the Liberty that was purchased for you, that belongs to you, that you are entitled to have as a glorious gift from God. I promise!"

I took an oath when I joined the military to support and defend the Constitution. I took an oath when I was sworn in as an attorney in the State of Florida to support and defend the Constitution. I took the same oath when I was sworn in as an Assistant State Attorney for Florida. I know that these oaths NEVER expire. That day, with those future leaders of America, I took another oath, one that will never expire, one that I will fight to keep to my very dying breath. This is why I do what I do. This is why my family and I travel all over the country. This is why I teach. This is what gives me purpose!

It is now our responsibility to pay this precious gift forward. America is not waiting for the return of our Founders. America is waiting for YOU to BECOME one.

Let us now STAND. For Liberty. For America. For our posterity.

11. Hope

Listening to the news and watching the headlines has become a habit, perhaps even an addiction, for the average Patriot. But I have come to realize that a daily diet of this is hazardous to our health. This never ending caustic supply of drama and crisis is not healthy for the body or the soul. There have been many in this battle for Liberty who have succumbed to the overwhelming negativity of the media-invented reality, leaving behind the battle to search for the "normal life."

We must guard against this intrusion and obstruction to the defense of Liberty. I am convinced the ever-continuing crisis after crisis is purposed to dishearten and discourage the patriot. So what is the solution? We must learn to find our hope and center ourselves on the true reality, not the one contrived by those receiving their marching orders from Alinsky, Cloward and Piven. We must know that just as we have inherited the Liberty we enjoy, we have also inherited the enemies of Liberty. We must pick up the mantle of those that came before us and learn from their courage and resolve.

Our history is rich with men and women who have surrendered all so that many could have the greatest nation the world has ever known. For over 700 years before the Declaration of Independence, men and women were learning the lessons that would be taught to our founders. Lessons that would infuse our founders with a courage and a hope that would build a nation focused upon Liberty.

Patrick Henry said, *"I have but one lamp by which my feet are guided, and that is the lamp of experience. I know no way to judge the future but by the past."*[163] He was letting us know that his knowledge of those last 700 years were the very reason he knew how this fight would turn out. He knew that every time men and women understood the value of Liberty and pledged all to protect it, they were always victorious. These guarantees of history must have raced through Henry's head: 1100 Charter of Liberties, Magna Carta, 1628 Petition of Right, 1641 Grand Remonstrance, and his very own Bill of Rights of 1689. These were battles fought in the name of Liberty and he knew that victory, while not easily attained, was guaranteed. This is our history. This is our guarantee. This is our victory!

Did these brave men and women live without fear? Hardly so! Mercy Otis Warren articulated this dilemma so well.

"I have my fears. Yet, notwithstanding the complicated difficulties that rise before us, there is no receding; May nothing ever check that glorious spirit of freedom which inspires the patriot in the cabinet and the hero in the field, with courage to maintain their righteous cause, and to endeavor to transmit the claim to posterity, even if they must seal the rich conveyance to their children with their own blood."[164]

They knew that bravery was not the absence of fear, but bravery is doing what you must even when you are afraid. They knew that the battle for Liberty, as Mercy called it, was a righteous cause. In a letter to her friend Mrs.

Macauley, in 1774, Mercy reveals the source of her strength. She said they were *"ready to sacrifice their devoted lives to preserve inviolate, and to convey to their children the inherent rights of men, conferred on all by the God of nature."*[165]

Our founders believed, as do I that the battle for Liberty is a battle for the gifts of God. Thomas Jefferson said, *"God who gave us life gave us liberty. Can the liberties of a nation be secure when we have removed a conviction that these liberties are the gift of God?"*[166]

For Patrick Henry, courage not only came from knowing the history that *"guided his feet"* or fighting with the *"vigilant, active, and the brave,"* but also knowing they served a *"just God who presides over the destinies of nations"* and when standing for Liberty, a gift from God, they could not fail.

He declared, *"We are three millions of people, armed in the holy cause of liberty, and in such a country as that which we possess, are invincible by any force which our enemy can send against us. Besides, sir, we shall not fight our battles alone. There is a just God who presides over the destinies of nations; and who will raise up friends to fight our battles for us."*[167]

The key to victory, the key to the courage that brings victory is not simply fighting the fight, but KNOWING we fight a righteous battle for the One who gave us that Liberty. There is strength in Certitude! Our founders were in a position to pledge their lives, the lives of their families, everything that they had because they were firmly rooted in ALL the assurances of Liberty. Our founders knew that

Liberty is a gift from God, and those that stand for God's gifts will be victorious through God's promises. They firmly believed that living in tyranny was worse than dying for Liberty. They knew that through their faith in God, their rewards in standing for God's gift would be certain, whether on the battlefield or beyond.

As Thomas Paine so eloquently put it, *"THESE are the times that try men's souls."*[168] But Paine's full statement gives a richness that is lost with the initial quote alone. Payne continues to tell us who will last in this battle and WHY they will last.

"The summer soldier and the sunshine patriot will, in this crisis, shrink from the service of their country; but he that stands by it now, deserves the love and thanks of man and woman. Tyranny, like hell, is not easily conquered; yet we have this consolation with us, that the harder the conflict, the more glorious the triumph. What we obtain too cheap, we esteem too lightly: it is dearness only that gives everything its value. Heaven knows how to put a proper price upon its goods; and it would be strange indeed if so celestial an article as FREEDOM should not be highly rated."[169]

If we wish to have the resolve that Mercy Otis-Warren spoke of or the confidence that Patrick Henry displayed, we must KNOW what Thomas Jefferson knew so we will not become the sunshine patriots Thomas Paine condemns. We must know Liberty is a gift from God. A gift with a high price is worth fighting for because God is with us.

This by far is not yet the darkest hour experienced by our nation. We still live in the greatest nation in the world, built upon the principles of Liberty. The principles cry all men are created equal and endowed by their Creator with certain inalienable rights. We live in a nation where all men have opportunity to life, Liberty, and the pursuit of happiness. No other nation can make that claim. No other people have that birth right. But with that gift comes great responsibility to secure that Liberty for generations to come. We cannot lose hope. We cannot let Liberty slip. Because, it is not **our** hope, it is not **our** Liberty, it is the hope and Liberty of ages and millions yet unborn. We must reacquaint ourselves with the lamp of experience that gives us the courage to see a guaranteed victory. But we must also reacquaint ourselves with the Giver of that gift of Liberty and the provider of the hope of victory.

In one of the darkest moments of our history, a story is told of Henry Wadsworth Longfellow. Henry's wife had been tragically and fatally burned in June of 1861. Henry, himself, was badly burned trying to put out the fire that consumed his beloved wife. He was so consumed by grief over the loss of his wife, at Christmas he wrote in his journal, *"How inexpressibly sad are all holidays."* One year later, Henry wrote, *"A merry Christmas' say the children, but that is no more for me."* That following year, Henry learns that his oldest son was severely wounded in the Civil War after a bullet passed under his shoulder blades damaging his spine. His journal was blank on Christmas on 1864. However, on Christmas day, 1865, Henry penned the words to "I Heard the Bells on Christmas Day".[170] During one of the darkest times our nation has ever known, Henry Wadsworth Longfellow found his hope;

"I heard the bells on Christmas Day
Their old familiar carols play,
And wild and sweet
The words repeat
Of peace on earth, good-will to men!
And thought how, as the day had come,
The belfries of all Christendom
Had rolled along
The unbroken song
Of peace on earth, good-will to men!
And in despair I bowed my head;
"There is no peace on earth," I said;
"For hate is strong,
And mocks the song
Of peace on earth, good-will to men!"
Then pealed the bells more loud and deep:
"God is not dead; nor doth he sleep!
The Wrong shall fail,
The Right prevail,
With peace on earth, good-will to men!"

Henry awoke from his despair and realized that God is not dead and is still the Giver of peace and hope. He knew that God promises victory to those who trust in Him and will stand for God's gifts. *"God is not dead; nor does he sleep! The Wrong shall fail; the Right prevail, With peace on earth, good-will to men!"*

That same promise belongs to us. We simply must place our trust in the right place. As a Christian I remind myself, that through the shed blood of Christ, whether the victory is on the battlefield or through the gates of Heaven, I am a winner either way. This is the REAL HOPE; a hope that can change the world.

Take Action

Here are **4** things you can do ***right now***

to help me ***fight for you!***

1

Visit **KrisAnneHall.Com**

And

JOIN the ***LIBERTY FIRST BRIGADE!***

2

Helps us in our endeavor to make our

Roots of Liberty Documentary Series

And pass on the truth to this and future generations.

Donate, Pray, Participate!

3

Get these books and get them into the hands of your neighbors, your family and your politicians

<u>Liberty First, The Path To Restoring America</u> 10 things every Patriot can do on the individual level to help restore America to its founding principles.

<u>Bedtime Stories for Budding Patriots</u> & <u>Essential Stories for Junior Patriots</u> Tools to teach children the fundamental truths about America.

4

Follow me on
Twitter at <u>@KrisAnneHall</u>
and on
Facebook at <u>www.facebook.com/krisanne.hall</u>

APPENDIX A

Nullification In A Nutshell

After perceiving a long train of usurpations of power by the federal government, which culminated in legislation known as Obamacare many Americans took to the streets in protest. They appealed to the Legislature to no avail. The legislation ultimately made its way to the Supreme Court. We then witnessed a colossal rewriting of our founding documents in the majority opinion to the Obamacare mandate. Justice John Roberts in a few lines pulled down the pillars of the Republic and set us on the path to totalitarianism.[171] Nearly half of the population rightfully regards this legislation as extending far beyond the enumerated powers of the federal government. The truth is, not only should the States be able to deal with their own health insurance issues, but the federal government has no legitimate authority to rule by such dictates. Yet, many who vowed to fight it "to the end" have now acquiesced and declared that it must be submitted to as "the law of the land." So is this the end? Since SCOTUS made its declaration from on high, must we now bow to an all-powerful government, from which no area of our daily life is off-limits? Or is there a remedy yet remaining? Can the States legitimately resist federal law or is this "treasonous" as some have suggested?

To answer these questions we must first understand the nature of the Republic we call the United States. These States are "United" in a compact, the Constitution. This compact, or contract, made among the States not only created the federal government but also dictated the limited and specific powers delegated to the federal government by the parties of this contract. Secondly, since the States are the parties to the compact and the creators of the central government, then the States, naturally, are the masters of their creation. That is to say, they are sovereign – independent of, separate from and sovereign **over** the federal government. All of the powers not delegated to the federal government remain with the States and the people. The 10th Amendment makes that very clear.

"The powers not delegated to the United States by the Constitution, nor prohibited by it to the States, are reserved to the States respectively, or to the people."[172] 10th Amendment

It is upon this foundation that the States have the ultimate right to stand against ANY unconstitutional law created or enforced by the federal government. The 10th Amendment declares that the federal government is to only operate within their delegated powers. James Madison explains those delegated powers in Federalist Paper 45:

"The powers delegated by the proposed Constitution to the federal government are few and defined. Those which are to remain in the State governments are numerous and indefinite. The former will be

exercised principally on external objects, as war, peace, negotiation, and foreign commerce…"[73]

*Madison then goes on to explain "the powers reserved to the several States will extend to **all the objects** which, in the **ordinary course of affairs**, concern the **lives, liberties**, and **properties** of the people, and the **internal order, improvement, and prosperity of the State.**"[74] (emphasis mine)*

Therefore, the 10th Amendment in conjunction with Madison's explanation makes it clear that the States' powers are numerous, the federal powers are few, and the federal government has no business interjecting itself into the powers reserved to the States. Claiming the 10th amendment says anything else would make the Constitution a complete absurdity.

Since there are no areas of power that are simply floating out in the neutral zone waiting for someone to use them, if the federal government uses a power that was not Constitutionally delegated, it must, without exception, steal it from the States. When the federal government does this, it removes power from the States, rights from the people, and makes the Constitution completely meaningless. Such overreach sets the precedent that no power is reserved to the States and that all power is open for federal taking. This effectively nullifies the 9th and 10th Amendments, and destroys the Constitutional barriers established to contain a limited and defined federal government. What will then be the federal government's limitations? Nothing but its own will.

*"That they will view this as seizing the rights of the States, and consolidating them in the hands of the general government, with a power assumed to bind the States, not merely in cases made federal, but in **all cases whatsoever**...that this would be **to surrender the form of government we have chosen**, and live under one **deriving its powers from its own will**, and not from our authority..."*[75] *(emphasis mine) Thomas Jefferson*

This is, in essence, what Justice Roberts declared in his opinion on Obamacare, overturning the very purpose of the Constitution itself – to enumerate the powers of a limited central government and bind it under the authority of the States. What happens when the barriers of the Constitution are completely swept away? The federal government will now have the ability to exercise any power over the States whatsoever. The people will be rendered completely powerless and irrelevant. What will be the purpose of elections then? We will no longer be a republic, but a government ruled as a Kingdom.

*"...for the federal government to **enlarge its powers** by **forced construction of the constitutional** charter **which defines them**...so as to destroy the meaning and effect of the particular enumeration which necessarily explains and limits the general phrases...**the obvious tendency and inevitable result**...would be, **to transform the present republican system** of the United States into an **absolute, or, at best, a mixed monarchy.**"*[76] *(emphasis mine) James Madison*

So, when the Legislative, Executive and Judicial branches of the federal government have collectively torn through the boundaries set by the Constitution, and the people have no recourse in the federal system, what is the remedy? What is the proper course when the federal government has gone rogue? The drafter of the Declaration of Independence, Thomas Jefferson and The Father of the Constitution, James Madison speak very clearly on the position of the States as the sovereign defenders of the foundations of our Republic. It is the founders of the Republic who must give us our remedy...

James Madison gives us this answer regarding the remedy to the States for combating federal overreach. In fact, according to our founders, it was not only the remedy but the DUTY of the States to stand in defense of the Republic.

"...in the case of deliberate, palpable, and dangerous exercise of other powers not granted...the states...**have the right, and are in duty bound, to interpose**, ...for maintaining, within their respective limits, the authorities, rights, and liberties..."[177] (emphasis mine) James Madison

What is this interposition? It is what Jefferson referred to as NULLIFICATION of the unauthorized acts of the federal government. It is the States declaring, "The federal government is NOT our master, the States and the people are the masters of the Constitution and we do not have to, nor will we comply!"

"Whenever the general government assumes undelegated powers, its acts are unauthoritative, void and of no force."[178] *(emphasis mine) Thomas Jefferson*

Nullification is the legitimate act of refusing to implement unconstitutional federal directives.

"That the several **states who formed [the Constitution]***, being sovereign and independent***, *have the unquestionable right to judge of its infraction; and,* **That a nullification***, by those sovereignties, of all unauthorized acts done under the color of that instrument,* **is the rightful remedy.***"*[179] *(emphasis mine) Thomas Jefferson*

To deny the States this right is tyrannical and is an unconstitutional doctrine. In fact our founders believed that if the States did not refuse to submit to unconstitutional use of federal power, the result would be the elimination of State powers, elimination of the rights of the people, and the complete dissolution of the Union and our Constitution.

"the doctrine which denies to the States the right of protecting their reserved powers, and which would vest in the General Government (it matters not through which department) the right of determining, exclusively and finally, the powers delegated to it, is incompatible with the sovereignty of the States, and of the Constitution itself, considered as the basis of the Federal Union."[180] *(emphasis mine) John C. Calhoun*

If the federal government uses a power that it was not delegated, it is unconstitutional by default. The federal government exists solely because of the Constitution. Therefore any act that is unconstitutional destroys the very legitimacy of the federal government's actions and therefore has no effect whatsoever. Since it has no effect, the States are merely declaring that fact, and are therefore not required to submit.

An epidemic of Constitutional ignorance has made it popular in our day to declare "this is the law of the land because the Supreme Court says so," and since SCOTUS has said "nullification is not valid," then it is not a proper remedy, some even claim that it is treasonous. The men who founded the nation found the assertion offensive that the Supreme Court had the ultimate authority to dictate to the States the acts of the federal government.

*"The idea that the general government is the exclusive judge of the extent of the powers delegated to it, stop **nothing short of despotism**- since the discretion of those who administer the government, and not the Constitution would be the measure of their powers."[181] (emphasis mine) Thomas Jefferson*

To assume that the Supreme Court has the final word on what will or will not be implemented throughout the land is to abandon all power of the States, and throw them into complete submission to federal power. It would be like allowing a criminal to determine his own guilt or innocence.

"If the decision of the judiciary be raised above the authority of the sovereign parties to the Constitution... dangerous powers, not delegated, may not only be usurped and executed by the other departments, but that the judicial department, also, may exercise or sanction dangerous powers beyond the grant of the Constitution... consequently, that the ultimate right of the parties to the Constitution, to judge whether the compact has been dangerously violated, must extend to violations by one delegated authority as well as by another—by the judiciary as well as by the executive, or the legislature."[182] (emphasis mine) James Madison,

Even the Federalist, Alexander Hamilton, made clear that the Constitution is binding upon every branch of the federal government. To suggest that the creature could overrule its creator was to our founders a complete absurdity.

"No legislative act, therefore, contrary to the Constitution, can be valid. To deny this, would be to affirm, that the deputy is greater than his principal; that the servant is above his master; that the representatives of the people are superior to the people themselves; that men acting by virtue of powers, may do not only what their powers do not authorize, but what they forbid."[183] Alexander Hamilton

It is incumbent upon the STATE REPRESENTATIVES to carry out their oath of office, "support and defend the Constitution of the United States" and be the guardians of the Liberty of its citizens. The Governors and Legislatures must draft a Resolution proclaiming the sovereignty of the

State and the unconstitutionality of the federal power and asserting the State's duty to deny said power. That Resolution must then be transmitted by the Governor to the Senators and Representatives representing the State in Congress.

In 1799 the legislators of Virginia new precisely what their responsibility was as representatives of the States and the people. They knew that their oath to support the Constitution was not just words or ceremony but a solemn obligation. To defend the Constitution they knew they had to *first* ensure the sovereignty of the States! To deny this obligation, they warned, would be deceitful and negligent and result in the federal government usurping the power that belongs to the States and to the people:

"Unwilling to shrink from our representative responsibilities...It would be [deceitful] in those entrusted with the GUARDIANSHIP OF THE STATE SOVEREIGNTY, and acting under the solemn obligation of the following oath, — "I do swear that I will support the Constitution of the United States," — not to warn you of encroachments, which, though clothed with the pretext of necessity, or disguised by arguments of expediency, may yet establish precedents which may ultimately devote a generous and unsuspicious people to all the consequences of usurped power."[184] *(emphasis mine) Address of the General Assembly to the People of the Commonwealth of Virginia, 1799*

When petition fails...when Congress refuses to enforce Separation of Powers and protect the sovereignty of the States...when the Supreme Court joins in the federal government's unconstitutional use of power, we cannot admit that revolution is the only solution that remains! Revolution does not save the Constitution, it can only destroy it. There must be another peaceful resolution; and there is: It is called Nullification. For the federal government or the States to deny this method of constitutional remedy is to say they are resolved to the destruction of the Constitution and the potential of driving its people to revolution.

"...*our Constitution is most worthless and tyrannical, if the usurpations of those who administer it, cannot be resisted by any means short of revolution. I have always considered the reserved powers of the States,* **as the only real check** *upon the powers of the federal government; and I have always considered it, not only the right, but the imperious duty of the States, so to apply that check, as not to dissolve the Union. And I have never been able to discover any mode of doing this, except by the positive refusal of the States to submit to usurpations...*"[185] *Judge Able P. Upshur (emphasis mine)*

"The acquiescence of the states, *under infractions of the federal compact,* **would either beget** *a speedy consolidation, by precipitating* **the state governments into impotency and contempt, or prepare the way for a revolution**, *by a repetition of these infractions until the people are aroused to appear in the majesty of their strength.*"[186] *(emphasis mine) Address of the General Assembly to the People of the Commonwealth of Virginia, 1799*

Therefore, in upholding their oath the States must stand against any legislation that serves to steal power from the

State. If the States fail to stand against this tyrannical use of power by the federal government, they will consent to their own destruction, or worse, to revolution.

Appendix B

Resolution

Of the Constitutional Sheriffs and Peace Officers Association

Pursuant to the powers and duties bestowed upon us by our citizens, the undersigned do hereby resolve that any Federal officer, agent, or employee, regardless of supposed congressional authorization, is required to obey and observe limitations consisting of the enumerated powers as detailed within Article 1 Section 8 of the U S Constitution and the Bill Of Rights.

The people of these united States are, and have a right to be, free and independent, and these rights are derived from the "Law of Nature and nature's God." As such, they must be free from infringements on the right to keep and bear arms, unreasonable searches and seizures, capricious detainments and every other natural right whether enumerated or not. (9th amendment)

We further reaffirm that "The powers not delegated to the United States by the Constitution, nor prohibited by it to the States, are reserved to the States respectively, or to the people." (10th amendment)

Furthermore, we maintain that no agency established by the U S Congress can develop its own policies or regulations which supersede the Bill of Rights or the Constitution, nor does the executive branch have the power to make law, overturn law or set aside law.

Therefore, in order to protect the American people, BE IT RESOLVED THAT,

The following abuses will not be allowed or tolerated:

1) Registration of personal firearms under any circumstances.

2) Confiscation of firearms without probable cause, due process, and constitutionally compliant warrants issued by a local or state jurisdiction.

3) Audits or searches of a citizen's personal affairs or finances without probable cause, due process, and constitutionally compliant warrants issued by a local or state jurisdiction.

4) Inspections of person or property without probable cause and constitutionally compliant warrants as required by the 4th Amendment and issued by a local or state jurisdiction.

5) The detainment or search of citizens without probable cause and proper due process compliance, or the informed consent of the citizen.

6) Arrests with continued incarcerations without charges and complete due process, including, but not limited to public and speedy jury trials, in a court of state or local jurisdiction.

7) Domestic utilization of our nation's military or federal agencies operating under power granted under the laws of war against American citizens.

8) Arrest of citizens or seizure of persons or property without first notifying and obtaining the express consent of the local sheriff.

AND, BE IT FURTHER RESOLVED,

that the undersigned Sheriffs, Peace Officers, and other Public Servants, do hereby denounce any acts or agencies which promote the aforementioned practices. All actions by the Federal Government and its agents will conform strictly and implicitly with the principles expressed within the United States Constitution, Declaration of Independence, and the Bill of Rights.

There is no greater obligation or responsibility of any government officer than to protect the rights of the people. Thus, any conduct contrary to the United States Constitution, Declaration of Independence, or the Bill of Rights will be dealt with as criminal activity.

ABOUT THE AUTHOR

KrisAnne Hall is a Constitutional attorney and former State prosecutor, fired after teaching the Constitution to conservative citizen groups - she would not sacrifice Liberty for a paycheck. She is a disabled veteran of the US Army, a former Russian linguist, a mother, a pastor's wife and a patriot. She now travels the country and teaching the Constitution and the history that gave us our founding documents.

Author of "Not a Living Breathing Document: Reclaiming Our Constitution", "Liberty First: The Path to Restoring American", and two student books; "Essential Stories For Junior Patriots" for middle and high school students, and "Bedtime Stories For Budding Patriots", a "read to me" book for non-readers. KrisAnne has also created a DVD series called, "The Roots of Liberty: The Historic Foundations of The Bill of Rights."

Born and raised in St. Louis, MO. She received her undergraduate degree in Bio-Chemistry from Blackburn College in 1991 and her J.D. from the University of Florida, Levin College of Law. KrisAnne now resides in North Florida with her husband JC (a pastor and former Russian instructor for the US Navy) and her adopted son Colton.

Here she is in her own words:

"Right up front there are some things that I need to tell you about myself. I want you to know where I came from and how I got to where I am today. I don't want to ever be accused of deception or dishonesty. So, in full disclosure:

I was not born a Constitutionalist. I did not live my life with an inherent understanding of Liberty and what is necessary to defend it. I was not raised a Christian. For some, these things will be a stumbling block, so you need to know from me.

I was raised a Democrat. The only thing more evil than Satan was a Republican in my home. There was no choices to be made in voting…straight Democrat party line was the only choice.

I was an environmentalist. An ardent environmentalist. Some of my best friends were members of Green Peace and I supported the WWF and PETA. I was a vegetarian by ideology, not for health reasons, for almost 15 years.

I believed in the "good" of scientific manipulations of food and the necessity of vaccines. Not only believed this, but helped create them when I was a biochemist for Monsanto.

I believed in Global Warming and defended it vigorously. I believed in the Big Bang and openly criticized those who believed in creationism as ignorant and misled.

I believed Government's duty and purpose was to be a provider for the people. I supported programs that would give the government more control over the people. I even believed a One World Government was the best way to go to ensure "global peace." I supported the principles of socialism, although I cannot claim to have known at the time it was socialism, per se, that I supported.

I supported abortion and often openly condemned others for being pro-life. I have argued with abortion protesters on street corners and called them names that I am not proud of.

I was not only not a Christian, but I practiced many other religions, including many occult versions. I was bitter against God and felt that only ignorant, weak people needed faith. I was too intelligent and too educated for such a feeble crutch.

I was not born with the knowledge that I have now. I did not wake up one morning with a divine epiphany. I traveled a long road. Learned some hard and painful lessons. My beliefs were challenged and I came to know the Truth.

I am able to stand firm on what I believe because I have discovered the difference between truth and lies. I am able to defend the truth because I walked the path. I can show you my path of discovery, and to be guaranteed it is not tied to any political motivation or personal gain...unless you call the liberation that comes from knowing the truth in the face of lies, a personal gain.

So when someone says to you..."Did you know that person used to be associated with this or that group or used to believe this... How can you possibly believe him now?" Remember this story.

It is good to question someone's "transformation". You SHOULD do that. If they cannot show you that path, step by step, you should question their motivations.

But do not discount someone's current position just because of who they USED to be or who they USED to associate with or what they USED to believe. Sometimes it is NOT a selfish or deceptive motivation, but a path to enlightenment. We all had to wake up somehow.

Just so you know where I stand." -KrisAnne Hall

KrisAnne is an incredibly passionate speaker - a true Patrick Henry of our time. She speaks to audiences all across the country on Constitutional History, American Exceptionalism, and the Fight for Liberty. Her passion and enthusiasm is contagious and she is able to inspire any group - a steadfast warrior in the Tea Party battle.

KrisAnne Hall's "The Roots of Liberty Seminar" is NOT JUST ANOTHER LECTURE ON THE CONSTITUTION. She presents the 700+ year history that gave us our founding documents – proving that our founding documents were not created on a whim and that they are reliable and relevant. It is important to know not only what your rights are, but why you have them.

In addition to the history of the Bill of Rights, KrisAnne presents each of the first ten amendments in their context –

in the words and history of our founders. She also presents the 17th amendment and what we must do to make our federal politicians accountable.

KrisAnne is a passionate speaker and has kept crowds attention for hours. This information is a must for all patriots and it must be passed on. If we are to reclaim our nation, we must reclaim our history!

The full seminar 5hrs (1hr segments). Partial Seminar also available.

KrisAnne is also available to present at regular meetings. Presentations last from 30 minutes to 1hr.

She is available to speak to your group, free of charge.

Citations

[1] John Adams (April 26, 1777) Personal Letter to Abigail Adams, para 8 at http://www.masshist.org/digitaladams/archive/doc?id=L17770426ja.

[2] Alexander Hamilton, *The Stand No. III* (April 7, 1798) para 4 at http://founders.archives.gov/documents/Hamilton/01-21-02-0233.

[3] Thomas Jefferson, as inscribed on the Jefferson Memorial, Washington D. C. National Park, taken from *A Summary View of the Rights of British America,* (August 1774) at http://avalon.law.yale.edu/18th_century/jeffsumm.asp and *Notes on the State of Virginia, Query XVIII,* (1784) at http://press-pubs.uchicago.edu/founders/documents/v1ch15s28.html.

[4] Benjamin Franklin, Addressing the Constitutional Convention (June 28, 1787) para 2 at http://www.constitution.org/primarysources/franklin.html.

[5] Patrick Henry, March 23, 1775, *Give Me Liberty*, at http://www.history.org/almanack/life/politics/giveme.cfm

[6] Thomas Jefferson (May 1, 1815) Personal letter to David Barrow, at http://seaofliberty.org/explore/jefferson-david-barrow/230.

[7] Daniel Webster, *An Anniversary Address Delivered by Daniel Webster Before the Federal Gentlemen of Concord and Its Vicinity, July 4, 1806*, The Granite Monthly, October 1881, vol. 5, page 7.

[8] James Madison, "Federalist 58" in *The Federalist Papers,* para. 7 at http://avalon.law.yale.edu/18th_century/fed58.asp.

[9] U.S. Const. art. 1, sec. 7.

[10] Alexander Hamilton, "Federalist 78" in *The Federalist Papers,* para. 11 at http://avalon.law.yale.edu/18th_century/fed78.asp.

[11] U.S. Const. art. 2 sec. 4.

[12] Thomas Jefferson, (August 18, 1821) personal letter to C. Hammond, para. 2 at http://rotunda.upress.virginia.edu/founders/default.xqy?keys=FOEA-print-04-02-02-2260.

[13] James Madison, "Federalist 45" in *The Federalist Papers,* para. 6 at http://avalon.law.yale.edu/18th_century/fed45.asp.

[14] English Bill of Rights, 1689, para. 2 at http://avalon.law.yale.edu/17th_century/england.asp.

[15] *How To Win Friends And Influence People*, Dale Carnegie, p. 36 (1936, Simon and Schuster).

[16] Declaration of Independence, July 4, 1776.

[17] Resolution introduced in the Continental Congress by Richard Henry Lee (Virginia) proposing a Declaration of Independence, June 7, 1776, at http://avalon.law.yale.edu/18th_century/lee.asp.

[18] John Adams, (July 3, 1776) personal letter to Abigail Adams, page 2 para. 3 at http://www.masshist.org/digitaladams/archive/doc?id=L17760703jasecond.

[19] Declaration of Independence, para. 6, July 4, 1776.

[20] Ibid.

[21] Ibid.

[22] U.S. Const., Preamble.

[23] Supra. at note 19.

[24] George Washington, *Farewell Address*, 1796, paragraphs 35-41 at http://avalon.law.yale.edu/18th_century/washing.asp.

[25] Thomas Jefferson, (Jan. 26, 1799) personal letter to Elbridge Gerry, para. 2 at http://www.let.rug.nl/usa/presidents/thomas-jefferson/letters-of-thomas-jefferson/jefl125.php.

[26] Supra, at note 24

[27] James Madison, Introduction to the Bill of Rights, The Annals of Congress, House of Representatives, First Congress, 1st Session, 448-460, 1789.

[28] Supra, at note 24.

[29] Thomas Jefferson, *Kentucky Resolution – Alien and Sedition Acts*, 1799, para. 4 at http://avalon.law.yale.edu/18th_century/kenres.asp.

[30] U.S. Articles of Confederation, art. II, 1781.

[31] Thomas Jefferson, (Jan. 26, 1811) personal letter to A.L.C. Destutt de Tracy, para. 4 at http://www.let.rug.nl/usa/presidents/thomas-jefferson/letters-of-thomas-jefferson/jefl209b.php.

[32] Thomas Jefferson (Dec. 23, 1791) personal letter to Archibald Stuart, para. 2 at http://www.let.rug.nl/usa/presidents/thomas-jefferson/letters-of-thomas-jefferson/jefl96.php.

[33] John Dickinson, *Letters of Fabius*, Letter III, 1788 pages 3-4 at http://deila.dickinson.edu/cdm/ref/collection/ownwords/id/247.

[34] Supra, at note 13.

[35] Supra, at note 19.

[36] U.S. Const., amend. X.

[37] Supra, at note 19.

[38] Ibid.

[39] Supra, at note 13.

[40] Ibid.

[41] Supra, at note 36.

[42] James Madison, *Virginia Resolution of 1798*, Dec. 24, 1798 para. 4 at http://www.constitution.org/cons/virg1798.htm.

[43] Ibid, at para. 7.

[44] Thomas Paine, *Common Sense, Thoughts On The Present State Of American Affiars*, para. 29 at http://www.ushistory.org/paine/commonsense/singlehtml.htm.

[45] Supra, at note 13.

[46] Supra, at note 29.

[47] Supra, at note 36.

[48] Supra, at note 42.

[49] Supra, at note 10.

[50] Supra, at note 19.

[51] Samuel Adams, *The Rights of the Colonists, The Report of the Committee of Correspondence to the Boston Town Meeting*, para. 1 (Nov. 20, 1772) at http://history.hanover.edu/texts/adamss.html.

[52] U.S. Const. amend. IX.

[53] Supra, at note 22.

[54] Supra, at note 51.

[55] Supra, at note 27.

[56] John C. Calhoun, *Fort Hill Address* (July 26, 1831) para. 3 at http://teachingamericanhistory.org/library/document/fort-hill-address/.

[57] James Madison, *Report on the Virginia Resolutions*, (Jan. 1800) para. 21 at http://press-pubs.uchicago.edu/founders/documents/v1ch8s42.html.e

[58] Ibid at para. 20.

[59] Letters From a Federal Farmer, *Letter XV*, (3 Jan. 18, 1788) para. At http://www.constitution.org/afp/fedfar15.htm.

[60] Thomas Jefferson, (March 9, 1821) personal letter to Judge Spencer Roane, para. 2 at http://www.yamaguchy.com/library/jefferson/1821.html.

[61] Supra, at note 29.

[62] Supra, at note 12.

[63] U.S. Const. art 6. cl 2.

[64] Supra, at note 56.

[65] Supra, at note 10.

[66] U.S. Const. art. 3 sec. 2. cl. 2, US Constitution.

[67] Supra, at note 57.

[68] James Madison, *Notes, On Nullification*, (Dec. 1834) para 9 at http://www.constitution.org/jm/18341200_nullification.htm.

[69] Ibid.

[70] Supra, at note 57.

[71] Kansas Secretary of State, Kris Kobach, speech given to the Kansas Tenth Amendment Center Annual Dinner, January 16, 2014.

[72] Supra, at note 51.

[73] James Madison, "Federalist 51" in *The Federalist Papers,* at http://avalon.law.yale.edu/18th_century/fed51.asp.

[74] Ibid.

[75] See www.CSPOA.org

[76] U.S. Const. amend. II.

[77] The General Records Schedule for Law Enforcement, Correctional Facilities, and District Medical Examiners, (Florida, 2013) Item 32.

[78] F.S.838.022 (1)

[79] Supra, at note 75.

[80] U.S. Const. art V.

[81] Thomas Jefferson (July 12, 1816) a personal letter to Samuel Kercheval, at http://oll.libertyfund.org/titles/808.

[82] James Madison, *Records of Federal Convention* citing Col. George Mason,

June 11, 1787 at http://press-pubs.uchicago.edu/founders/documents/a5s2.html.

[83] Supra, at note 5.

[84] James Madison, *Records of the Federal Convention*, Sept. 10, 1787 at http://press-pubs.uchicago.edu/founders/documents/a5s2.html.

[85] James Madison, *Copy In Substance Of A Letter To G. L. Turberville, Esq.*, Nov 2, 1788 at http://oll.libertyfund.org/titles/1937.

[86] James Madison, "Federalist 49" in *The Federalist Papers,* at http://avalon.law.yale.edu/18th_century/fed49.asp.

[87] Ibid.

[88] Supra, at note 79.

[89] Thomas H. Neale, Congressional Research Service, *The Article V Convention to Propose Constitutional Amendments: Contemporary Issues for Congress.* July 9, 2012 (www.crs.gov R42589) pages 2-3.

[90] Ibid, page 4.

[91] Ibid.

[92] Ibid, page 8.

[93] Alexander Hamilton, "Federalist 85" in *The Federalist Papers,* at http://avalon.law.yale.edu/18th_century/fed85.asp.

[94] Supra, at note 84.

[95] Ibid, page 9.

[96] Ibid.

[97] Ibid.

[98] James Madison, *Record of the Federal Convention,* citing Col. George Mason, Sept 15, 1787 at http://press-pubs.uchicago.edu/founders/documents/a5s2.html.

[99] Supra, at note 79.

[100] Supra, at note 84, page 11.

[101] Ibid.

[102] Ibid, page 12.

[103] Ibid, page 13.

[104] Ibid, page 14.

[105] Ibid, page 18.

[106] Ibid.

[107] Ibid.

[108] Ibid.

[109] Ibid, page 20.

[110] U.S. Const., art 1 sec 7 cl 3.

[111] Supra, at note 84, page 26.

[112] Ibid.

[113] Ibid, page 29.

[114] Ibid.

[115] Ibid.

[116] Goldwater Institute, "Compact for a Balanced Budget," at http://goldwaterinstitute.org/article/compact-balanced-budget.

[117] Thomas H. Neale, Congressional Research Service, *The Article V Convention to Propose Constitutional Amendments: Contemporary Issues for Congress.* April 11, 2014.

[118] Constitution, Article 1 section 10 clause 3.

[119] Samuel Adams, May 15, 1764, Boston Record Commissioners' Report, vol. 16, pp. 120-122.

[120] Ibid.

[121] James Otis, Jr. *Against Writs of Assistance,* February 24, 1761 at para. 3 www.constitution.org/bor/otis_against_writs.htm.

[122] Ibid.

[123] John Adams (March 29, 1817) Personal letter to William Tudor, *Works of John Adams, Second President of the United States,* (Little, Brown and company, 1856) vol. 10, page 247 para. 5.

[124] Supra, at note 112.

[125] Samuel Adams, *Petition to the Selectmen of this Town*, Boston-Gazette and Country Journal, No. 918, (October 26, 1772) at http://www.masshist.org/revolution/doc-viewer.php?item_id=483&old=1&mode=nav.

[126] The Boston Committee of Correspondence, *The Votes and Proceedings of the Freeholders and other Inhabitants of the Town of Boston, In Town Meeting Assembled,* (Edes, and Gill, in Queen Street, and T. and J. Fleet, in Cornhill, 1772) at http://www.masshist.org/revolution/doc-viewer.php?item_id=609.

[127] Boston Port Act, March 31, 1774 (enacted June 1, 1774) at http://avalon.law.yale.edu/18th_century/boston_port_act.asp.

[128] Declaratory Act, March 18, 1766 at http://avalon.law.yale.edu/18th_century/declaratory_act_1766.asp.

[129] Thomas Gage, Royal Governor of Massachusetts, 1774 at http://www.mass.gov/portal/government-taxes/laws/interactive-state-house/historical/governors-of-massachusetts/royal-colony-of-massachusetts-1692-1774/thomas-gage-1774.html.

[130] Earl of Dartmouth (April, 9th 1774) Personal letter to Governor Gage, at http://lincoln.lib.niu.edu/cgi-bin/amarch/getdoc.pl?/var/lib/philologic/databases/amarch/.156.

[131] From the John Rowe diaries, (September 1-4, 1774) p. 1901 at http://www.masshist.org/revolution/image-viewer.php?item_id=495&img_step=1&tpc=&pid=2&mode=transcript&tpc=&pid=2#page1.

[132] Earl of Dartmouth, (October 17, 1774) Personal letter to Governor Gage at http://lincoln.lib.niu.edu/cgi-bin/amarch/getdoc.pl?/var/lib/philologic/databases/amarch/.1006.

[133] Governor Gage, (December 15, 1774) Personal letter to the Earl of Dartmouth, at http://lincoln.lib.niu.edu/cgi-bin/amarch/getdoc.pl?/var/lib/philologic/databases/amarch/.1265.

[134] Documents Relating to the Colonial, Revolutionary and Post-revolutionary History of the State of New Jersey, *Circular Letter from the Earl of Dartmouth To All The Governors in America…*, October 19, 1774 (New Jersey Historical Society, 1886) pp. 497-498.

[135] Resolutions of the Provincial Congress of Virginia, March 23, 1774 at http://avalon.law.yale.edu/18th_century/res_cong_va_1775.asp.

[136] Thomas Paine, *Common Sense, Thoughts on the Present State of American Affairs,* (3d, ed., 1776) at http://www.ushistory.org/paine/commonsense/singlehtml.htm.

[137] The Grand Remonstrance, Presented to King Charles I, (December 1, 1641) at http://www.constitution.org/eng/conpur043.htm.

[138] Supra, at note 51.

[139] Sheriff Jim Coats, testimony before the Florida House of Representatives, April 11, 2011 (video) at http://youtu.be/pqrLRePn8Js.

[140] Emily Miller, *Smoking gun exposed – D.C. police chief covers up giving Feinstein illegal "assault weapons"*, Washington Times, Wednesday, October 9, 2013, at http://www.washingtontimes.com/news/2013/oct/9/miller-how-a-senator-got-her-guns-for-a-dc-show-an/?page=all.

[141] George Mason, Debate in Virginia Ratifying Convention, (June 14, 1788) at http://press-pubs.uchicago.edu/founders/documents/a1_8_12s27.html.

[142] Noah Webster, *Examination of the Leading Principles of the Federal Constitution, 1787*, (October 10, 1787) p. 43 at http://www.potowmack.org/2noahweb.html#top.

[143] Letter XVIII, *Letters from the Federal Farmer,* (January 25, 1788) para 4 at http://www.constitution.org/afp/fedfar18.htm.

[144] Patrick Henry, Debate in Virginia Ratifying Convention, (June 5-6, 1788) para 4 at http://press-pubs.uchicago.edu/founders/documents/a5s9.html.

[145] Supra, at note 51.

[146] Supra, at note 5.

[147] Supra, at note 51.

[148] Supra, at note 16.

[149] Samuel Adams, Boston Gazette (February 27, 1769) quoting Justice Blackstone, at http://press-pubs.uchicago.edu/founders/print_documents/v1ch3s4.html.

[150] Ibid.

[151] Alexander Hamilton, "Federalist 33" in *The Federalist Papers,* at http://avalon.law.yale.edu/18th_century/fed33.asp.

[152] James Madison, "Federalist 46" in *The Federalist Papers,* at http://avalon.law.yale.edu/18th_century/fed46.asp.

[153] Thomas Jefferson (Feb 22, 1787) Personal letter to Abigail Adams, at http://www.let.rug.nl/usa/presidents/thomas-jefferson/letters-of-thomas-jefferson/jefl55.php.

[154] Samuel Adams, writing as Candidus, Essay in the Boston Gazette, Oct. 14, 1771 at http://www.thefederalistpapers.org/founders/samuel-adams/samuel-adams-writing-as-candidus-essay-in-the-boston-gazette-oct-14-1771.

[155] Supra, at note 133.

[156] Supra, at note 135.

[157] Mercy Otis Warren, *History of the rise, progress, and termination of the American Revolution,* printed by Manning and Loring, For E. Larkin, No. 47, Cornhill, 1805, page 431.

[158] Supra, at note 5.

[159] Letters From a Federal Farmer, *Letter VI,* (3 Jan. 18, 1788) para. At http://www.constitution.org/afp/fedfar6.htm.

[160] Ibid

[161] Rep. Mike Rogers, (Mi), Intelligence Committee Chairman, October 29, 2013 testimony at http://www.c-span.org/video/?c4470916/mike-rogers-view-privacy.

[162] Alexander Hamilton, *A Full Vindication,* The Papers of Alexander Hamilton, Harold C. Syrett, ed. Columbia University Press, 1961, page 69.

[163] Supra, at note 5.

[164] Mercy Otis Warren (August 2, 1775) Personal Letter to John Adams.

[165] Mercy Otis Warren (December 29, 1774) Personal Letter to Catharine Macaulay, at http://www.digitalhistory.uh.edu/exhibits/dearmadam/letter2.html.

[166] Supra, at note 3.

[167] Supra, at note 5.

[168] Thomas Paine, *The Crisis,* December 23, 1776, at http://www.ushistory.org/paine/crisis/c-01.htm.

[169] Ibid.

[170] Tom Stewart, *I Heard the Bells on Christmas Day,* December 20, 2001 at http://www.lavenderway.com/story_behind.htm.

[171] KrisAnne Hall, *Justice Roberts Gives Some Good Advice,* June 30, 2012 at http://krisannehall.com/justice-roberts-gives-some-good-advice/.

[172] Supra, at note 36.

[173] Supra, at note 13.

[174] Ibid.

[175] Supra, at note 25.

[176] Supra, at note 57.

[177] Ibid.

[178] Supra, at note 25.

[179] Ibid.

[180] Supra, at note 56.

[181] Supra, at note 25.

[182] Supra, at note 56.

[183] Supra, at note 10.

[184] Address of the General Assembly to the People of the Commonwealth of Virginia, Attest: John Steward, C.H.D, Agreed to by Senate January 23, 1799, true copy from the original deposited in the office of General Assembly, at http://oll.libertyfund.org/titles/1941.

[185] Judge Able P. Upshur, written under the pseudonym "Locke", *An Exposition of the Virginia Resolutions of 1798 (No. I),* The Examiner and Journal of Political Economy, vol. II, no. 4. Wednesday, September 17, 1834.

[186] Supra, at note 175.

37917314R00113

Made in the USA
San Bernardino, CA
28 August 2016